KEY CONCEPTS FOR THE FASHION INDUSTRY

Understanding Fashion series

ISSN 1753-3406

Series Editors:
Alison Goodrum, Manchester Metropolitan University, UK
Kim Johnson, University of Minnesota, USA

Understanding Fashion is a series of short, accessible, authored books designed to provide students with a map of the fashion field. The books are aimed at beginning undergraduate students and they are designed to cover an entire module. Accessibly written, each book will include boxed case studies, bullet point chapter summaries, guides to further reading, and questions for classroom discussion. Individual titles can be used as a key text or to support a general introductory survey. They will be of interest to students studying fashion from either an applied or cultural perspective.

Titles in the series include:

Fashion Design
Elizabeth Bye

Fashion and the Consumer
Jennifer Yurchisin and Kim K.P. Johnson

Fashion Trends: Analysis and Forecasting
Eundeok Kim, Ann Marie Fiore and Hyejeong Kim

KEY CONCEPTS FOR THE FASHION INDUSTRY

Andrew Reilly

B L O O M S B U R Y
LONDON • NEW DELHI • NEW YORK • SYDNEY

Bloomsbury Academic
An imprint of Bloomsbury Publishing Plc

50 Bedford Square	1385 Broadway
London	New York
WC1B 3DP	NY 10018
UK	USA

www.bloomsbury.com

Bloomsbury is a registered trade mark of Bloomsbury Publishing Plc

First published 2014

British Library Cataloguing-in-Publication Data
A catalogue record for this book is available from the British Library.

ISBN: HB: 978-0-8578-5364-6
PB: 978-0-8578-5365-3
ePDF: 978-0-8578-5366-0
ePub: 978-0-8578-5367-7

Library of Congress Cataloging-in-Publication Data
Reilly, Andrew Hinchcliffe.
Key concepts for the fashion industry / Andrew Reilly.
pages cm — (Understanding fashion series, ISSN 1753-3406)
Includes bibliographical references and index.
ISBN 978-0-85785-365-3 (pbk.) — ISBN 978-0-85785-364-6 (hardback) —
ISBN 978-0-85785-366-0 (ePDF) — ISBN 978-0-85785-367-7 (ePUB)
1. Fashion. 2. Clothing trade. 3. Fashion merchandising. I. Title.
TT507.R389 2014
746.9'2—dc 3
2013050286

Typeset by RefineCatch Limited, Bungay, Suffolk

CONTENTS

List of Illustrations   viii
Acknowledgements   x

1   **Overview**   1
    Introduction to theory   1
    Why use theory?   9
    Methods of inquiry   10
    What is fashion?   12
    Who has fashion?   14
    Fashioning the body   16
    The tipping point   18
    Semiotics   19
    Modern, postmodern, post-postmodern   19
    Organization of text   23
    Boxed case 1.1: Rudd/Lennon model of body aesthetics   25
    Boxed case 1.2: Maslow's hierarchy and fashion   26
    Boxed case 1.3: Fashion is a meme   26
    Summary   27
    Key Terms   27
    Discussion questions   28
    Learning activities   28
    Notes   28
    Further reading   29

2   **Fashion and the Individual**   31
    The Public, Private, and Secret Self   33
    Body image   35
    Aesthetic perception and learning   38
    Shifting Erogenous Zones   40
    Historic Continuity theory   45
    Symbolic Interaction theory   47
    Boxed case 2.1: One individual starts a trend   49
    Boxed case 2.2: Fashion leaders: Celebrities and fashion   51
    Summary   52
    Key Terms   52
    Discussion questions   52
    Learning activities   53
    Further reading   53

3 **Fashion and Society**   55
   Trickle Down theory   57
   Trickle Up theory   62
   Scarcity/Rarity   64
   Conspicuous consumption   68
   Political use of fashion   71
   Boxed case 3.1: Cinderella's glass slipper   75
   Boxed case 3.2: Ethics focus: The diamond monopoly   76
   Summary   76
   Key Terms   77
   Discussion questions   77
   Learning activities   77
   Notes   78
   Further reading   78

4 **Fashion and Culture**   79
   Zeitgeist   80
   Spatial diffusion   84
   Subcultural or style tribes/collective behavior   86
   Cultural authentication   90
   Fashion as modernity   92
   Boxed case 4.1: Yakuza as subcultural style and spatial
      diffusion   96
   Boxed case 4.2: Ethics focus: Akihiko Izukura   97
   Summary   98
   Key Terms   98
   Discussion questions   98
   Learning activities   98
   Notes   99
   Further reading   99

5 **The Fashion System**   101
   Market Infrastructure theory   102
   Trickle Across theory   103
   Innovation theory   104
   Historic resurrection   107
   Branding   110
   Boxed case 5.1: Ethics focus: Knock-offs   113
   Boxed case 5.2: New technology of body fashions   116
   Summary   116
   Key Terms   116
   Discussion questions   117
   Learning activities   117
   Notes   117
   Further reading   117

6 **Conclusion**   119
   One phenomenon, many theories   120
   Fashion blunders   121
   Boxed case 6.1: Ethics focus: Offensive fashion   125
   Boxed case 6.2: Classics can have fashionable details too   126
   Summary   128
   Discussion questions   128
   Learning activities   128
   Notes   129
   Further reading   129

Bibliography   131
Index   139

CONTENTS

ILLUSTRATIONS

Chapter 1

1.1	Man wearing a suit backwards	3
1.2	The stock market and hemlines	7
1.3	The fashion life-cycle	14
1.4	Panier and corset from the 18th century	17
1.5	Cartoon lampooning the semiotic nature of dress	20
1.6	*Reverie* by Roy Lichtenstein	21
1.7	Bracelet made from children's Matchbox cars	22
1.8	The Rudd/Lennon model of body aesthetics	25

Chapter 2

2.1	Unique styles can ignite a trend	32
2.2	Damhorst's model of the many influences on clothing meaning	39
2.3	The Theory of Shifting Erogenous Zones: the back	41
2.4	The Theory of Shifting Erogenous Zones: the shoulder	42
2.5	The Theory of Shifting Erogenous Zones: the leg	43
2.6	Graph illustrating the width of men's jacket lapels in the 20th century	46
2.7	The Nivi style of sari	50
2.8	Reb'l Fleur by singer Rihanna	51

Chapter 3

3.1	Man exhibiting bad taste by wearing socks with sandals	56
3.2	The fashion of the Teddy Boys	60
3.3	Levi Strauss denim jeans were the work wear of miners in 1882	63
3.4	This bracelet is considered valuable because it is made with diamonds	65
3.5	The Halston brand lost value when Halston III for J. C. Penney was offered to consumers	67
3.6	Luxury designer brands are recognized as being expensive	69
3.7	The Sans Culottes of the French Revolution were identified by their clothing	73

Chapter 4

4.1 The Amish wear traditional clothes that do not change from
season to season   80
4.2 This 1949 Dior ensemble was made in the New Look style   82
4.3 Marc Jacobs' grunge collection for Perry Ellis   85
4.4 The cast of the American television series "Jersey Shore"   87
4.5 The fashionable Australian Akubura hat and oil-cloth jacket   89
4.6 This comic by Jen Sorensen illustrates the irony of the Nerd or
Geek Chic style   90
4.7 This holokū from the 1900s exemplifies the concept of cultural
authentication   93
4.8 Yakuza-style irezumi sleeves demonstrate a fashion trend   97

Chapter 5

5.1 The availability of cultured pearls made them a classic
wardrobe staple   106
5.2 Fashion designers often look to the past: 1890s men's shoes   108
5.3 Fashion designers often look to the past: Varvatos shoes in
the late 2000s   108
5.4 Gap returned to their iconic blue and white logo after a new
logo backlash   112
5.5 The unique design of the Hermès Birkin bag   114
5.6 Hermès Birkin bag knock-offs   115

Chapter 6

6.1 Princesses Eugenie and Beatrice of York were ridiculed for
their wedding hats   124
6.2 The keffiyeh scarf became a controversial fashion item   125
6.3 Converse shoes often have fashionable elements that change   127
6.4 Details from three trench coats   127

ACKNOWLEDGEMENTS

The author recognizes the following people for their involvement in helping to produce this book: Dr. Kim K. P. Johnson, for asking me to write a proposal on fashion theory for the Understanding Fashion series; Marcia Morgado for her patience with my endless question, "does this make sense?"; Dr. Attila Pohlmann for his assistance with photography; Dr. Barbara (Bobbie) Yee, chair of the Department of Family and Consumer Sciences at the University of Hawai'i, Mānoa, for her support of my writing; all team members at Bloomsbury Academic (formerly Berg) for their guidance, suggestions, and patience, including Anna Wright, Hannah Crump, and Emily Roessler; and my mother, Judith Charboneau, father, Terry Reilly, brother, Noah Reilly, my grandparents, Bill and Doris Hinchcliffe, and dog Holly for their continued support of my career.

The author and publisher gratefully acknowledge the permission granted to reproduce the copyright material in the book.
Nata Aha/Shutterstock.com
Anne Bissonnette
S_buckley/Shutterstock.com
Roz Chast/The New Yorker Collection/www.cartoonbank.com
Mary Lynn Damhorst
Fairchild Books
Mark Hamilton
Natali Glado/Shutterstock.com
International Textile and Apparel Association
Kim Miller-Spillman
Lobke Peers/Shutterstoc.com
Levi Strauss & Company, San Francisco
Estate of Roy Lichtenstein
Joseph McKeown
George Chinsee/WWD © Condé Nast 1992
Helga Esteb/Shutterstock.com
Dominique Maitre/WWD © Condé Nast 2009
Christopher Meder – Photography/Shutterstock.com
Northfoto/Shutterstock.com
The Ohio State University Historic Costume and Textiles Collection
Paffy/Shutterstock.com

Tony Palmieri/WWD © Condé Nast 1984
Attila Pohlmann
Josephine Schiele/Lucky © Condé Nast
Pascal Le Segretain/Getty Images
Jen Sorensen
Vladyslav Starozhylov/Shutterstock.com
University of Hawai'i Historic Costume Museum
Victoria and Albert Museum, London
Greg Ward NZ/Shutterstock.com
Julie Whitehead
Billy Whitney, 808 Tattoo

Every effort has been made to trace copyright holders and to obtain their permission for the use of copyright material. This publisher apologizes for any errors or omissions in the above list and would be grateful if notified of any corrections that should be incorporated into future reprints to editions of this book.

1

OVERVIEW

Introduction to theory

In Paris a fashion designer is sketching a new collection. At a convention in Las Vegas a buyer is looking among more than one thousand vendors to select dresses to sell in a boutique in Miami. In London a forecaster is analyzing data to predict the fashion trends three years from now. In Shanghai a merchandiser is preparing a report to propose the fashion direction for a popular chain of budget-priced retail stores throughout Asia. Each of these people is an expert in their field and each person will use a framework or principles of fashion to guide their decisions. The fashion designer will lower the hemline of dresses by two inches because she understands the directional nature of fashion. The buyer will scout for merchandise that is unique and exclusive because his customers desire to look different from other people. The forecaster will examine the social movements to make a prediction because she understands how society impacts trends. And, the merchandiser will flood the market with a few styles because he understands that if businesses offer a limited number of styles there is greater chance of them becoming a **trend**. Each of these people makes logical choices based on established principles and concepts of fashion.

The word **theory** is derived from the ancient Greek word *theoria* which meant "to look at or view." Greek philosophers would "look at" a situation and try to find an explanation for it. In scientific terms today theories are a framework for thinking about, examining, or interpreting something. Consider the following definitions of theory:

- "A theory consists of a conceptual network of propositions that explain an observable phenomenon" (Lillethun, 2007, 77).
- "A systematic explanation for the observations that relate to a particular aspect of life" (Babbie, 2004, G11).
- "A set of interrelated constructions (variables), definitions, and propositions that presents a systematic view of phenomena by specifying relations among variables, with the purpose of explaining natural phenomena" (Kerlinger, 1979, p. 64).

- "An idea or set of ideas that is intended to explain facts or events; an idea that is suggested or presented as possibly true but that is not known or proven to be true" (Merriam-Webster, 2013a, n.p.).
- "A contemplative and rational type of abstract or generalized thinking or the results of such thinking" (Wikipedia, 2013, n.p.).

We can examine behaviors, actions, occurrences, works, and any other tangible or intangible phenomena. Theories are made of different parts that contribute to the total understanding. Part of the theory might be true while other parts might not have support, but it does not necessarily change the theory as a whole. "Like fashion itself, the theories that explain fashion movement are constantly revised and refined" (Brannon, 2005, p. 82). By analogy, a garment that is made up of a bodice, skirt, collar, sleeves, and cuffs is called a **dress**. However, if you take off the cuffs it is still called a dress, or if you add a pocket it is still a dress. Changing part of the whole does not invalidate the whole.

Theories are divided into three categories based on their scope of explanation: grand, middle-range, and substantive (Merriam, 1988). Grand theories are very broad, all-inclusive, universal and are useful for organizing other ideas; they offer general ideas, such as Albert Einstein's Theory of Relativity. Middle-range theories do not attempt to explain such overarching phenomenon as do grand theories but rather concentrate on limited phenomena; one could argue that the theory of collective behavior (i.e., that fashion trends are inspired by specific groups of people with unique aesthetic styles; further explained in Chapter 4) is a middle-range theory. And substantive theories offer ideas and reasons in a narrow setting, such as the reasons for Japanese immigrants to adopt westernized **clothing** in Honolulu, Hawai'i in the 1920s.

Theories often come from concepts or laws. A **concept** is a general abstract idea; the idea of **fashion**—adoption of trends for a specific time period—is a concept. A **law** is a simple, basic description of phenomena that is undoubtedly true. The explanation of or why the phenomena occurs is a theory. A theory surmises or postulates why it happens. A theory is sometimes referred to as a **theoretical framework**. This is different from a **conceptual framework**, where the specific relationships between variables are detailed. A conceptual framework is nested within or based on the theoretical framework. For example, a theoretical framework might be that people tattoo their bodies to mark rites of passage. A conceptual framework will use this theory and examine specific variables—how do age, social rank, economics, and gender affect tattooing? Throughout this text you will find many examples of theoretical frameworks and conceptual frameworks.

Theories are developed from hypotheses. Hypotheses are educated guesses based on observation. Hypotheses can never be proven, only supported or rejected. When a **hypothesis** has been supported by numerous tests it becomes a theory. There is no guideline as to how many tests it takes to transform a hypothesis into a theory; rather, that decision is left up to the community studying it after they have determined they have exhausted all possible variations of the hypothesis.

Figure 1.1 Why is this man wearing a suit backwards? Is this a new aesthetic trend? Is this a protest? Is this a sign of postmodernity? Theory will help to answer questions like these and explain the reason for this peculiar display of dress. Iulian Valentin.

In a very general sense, we can say that "people wear clothing in civilized societies" is a law. The explanations why people wear clothing can constitute a theory. The ideas that test or support the theory are hypotheses that are accepted or rejected. You will see in the following example that with each level, the wording is more specific; it is moving from abstract to concrete.

Concept: Fashion—group adoption of a trend during a specific time period.
Law: People in civilized societies wear clothing.
Theory: People wear clothing due to climate conditions.
Hypothesis 1: As temperatures drop, people will wear more layers of clothing.
Hypothesis 2: As temperatures increase, people will wear fewer layers of clothing.
Hypothesis 3: The change in temperature will have no effect on the number of layers of clothing that people wear.

In order to test the hypothesis, you record temperatures in a given area and ask people how many layers of clothing they are wearing. When you analyze your data you find that when temperatures dropped, people added more layers of clothing, and conversely, when temperatures increased people wore fewer layers of clothing. Therefore, you accept hypotheses 1 and 2 but reject hypothesis 3. As a result you have found evidence that supports your theory that people wear clothing due to climate conditions. Other people may subsequently test the theory and find additional support, such as different types of clothes are worn during different climate conditions (e.g., rain, snow, drought) and therefore add to the body of knowledge about climate and clothing.

Models try to predict phenomena, based on theoretical framework, and are often represented as a diagram. A model can detail direction, interaction, and choices. Models can be based on theoretical or conceptual frameworks. The Rudd/Lennon Model of Body Aesthetics described in this chapter is an example of a model that summarizes the steps and decisions a person experiences when creating a personal aesthetic or "look."

A **taxonomy** is a system of classification. In the Animal Kingdom, animals are divided into invertebrate and vertebrate, then further divided within those groups (vertebrate are further divided into fish, reptiles, amphibians, birds, mammals). Pets can be divided into categories (cats, dogs, birds) and then further with each group (short hair, long hair; breed; indoors, outdoors). Even your wardrobe can be divided using a taxonomy: casual, professional, special occasion, etc.; within those categories you can further divide them by color, price, and frequency of wearing. The purpose of a taxonomy is that it helps organize data based on similar qualities or characteristics to find commonalities, differences, and gaps. You may find that your wardrobe taxonomy informs you that you have an overabundance of special occasion clothes but not enough professional clothes. The Public, Private, and Secret Self is an example of a taxonomy that classifies clothing according to type of dress by level of self-expression and will be further detailed in Chapter 2.

Some explanations of phenomena are revised until an adequate theory is found. The theory of gravity was altered over centuries, with additions and revisions from Aristotle in 300 BC, Galileo Galilei during the European Renaissance, Sir Isaac Newton in the 17th century, and Albert Einstein in the last century.

Some theories compete with each other to explain the same phenomena. In trying to explain why people commit crime, a number of theories have emerged, including phrenology (the measurement of cranial features where dimensions indicate criminal capacity; since abandoned as a legitimate theory); biological causes (e.g., bad genes); social causes (e.g., poverty, education; group affiliation); psychological causes (e.g., childhood abuse); and environmental or ecological causes (e.g., isolated or darkened areas).

There are also competing theories regarding the original purposes of clothing. Historic evidence provides material products that can be interpreted through different lenses. Pierced marine snail shells 75,000 years old were found in a cave on Blombos, South Africa (d'Errico, Henshilwood, Vanhaeren, & Niekerk, 2005; Vanhaeren, d'Errico, van Niekerk, Henshilwood & Erasmus, 2013). Also found in the Blombos cave was ochre (Henshilwood, d'Errico, Yates, et al., 2002; Henshilwood, d'Errico, & Watts, 2009). The snail shells were pierced as if to tie on a string and ochre likely was used to decorate the body in pre-historic times (Schildkrout, 2001), therefore it is suggested that the items were used for personal adornment. In addition, a pendant in the shape of a horse carved from mammoth tusk was found in Germany and believed to be 32,000 years old.

Needles made of bone and ivory, 30,000 years old, were found in Russia (Hoffecker & Scott, 2002; Dorey, 2013), suggesting they were used to sew animal skins, animal fur, or fabrics together. Flax fibers found to be from 34,000 BC were found in an ancient cave in the Eurasian country of Georgia and surmised to be evidence of baskets and clothing (Kvavadze, Bar-Yosef, Belfer-Cohen, et al., 2009). Some of the oldest clothing items were found in contemporary Denmark and dated to the early Bronze Age (2900–2000 BC) (Boucher, 1987). These items were made of woven cloth and included sewn bodices, tunics, hats, belts, and a skirt.

While we know that clothing and personal adornment has existed for many millennia, the reason for their creation is debated. Many theories speculate about their original purpose(s). Greeks and Chinese believed the original function of clothing was to protect the body from weather and natural elements while other people (such as psychologists, religious scholars, etc.) argue that clothing developed to provide modesty, for magical purposes, or to be aesthetically pleasing (Boucher, 1987). Boucher writes:

> [W]e may at least surmise that when the first men covered their bodies to protect themselves from the climate, they also associated their primitive garments with the idea of some magical identification in the same way that their belief in sympathetic magic spurred them to paint the walls of their caves with representations of successful hunting. After all, some primitive peoples who normally lived naked feel the need to clothe themselves on special occasions. (p. 9)

Boucher has noted the existence of five general categories of clothing: draped, slip-on, closed sewn, open sewn, and sheath. (In the modern period these types began to become interbred and new composite categories emerged.) Boucher, therefore, argues that while clothing can inspire fear or establish authority or project an image of power, because these types existed in different cultures and different discrete civilizations, something other than politics, race, or religion had to influence design—climate and geography. Thus, it is likely that the original purpose of clothing was for protection.

In 1991 a frozen man was found in the Ötztal Alps and nicknamed "Frozen Fritz." Fritz dates from 3300 BC and the ice preserved portions of his clothing and body. At the time of his death he was wearing a coat, belt, belt pouch, leggings, and shoes made of leather, all of which had been sewn. Also found was a cloak constructed from grass woven together. In addition to his apparel, Fritz's body was marked with tattoos that coincided with acupuncture points for ailments that Fritz experienced. It was therefore hypothesized that some of the tattoos were used for health purposes. Thus, while Fritz's clothing may have been for climate purposes, his body adornment may have been for health.

The reasons for these changes in theory or alternative explanations are due to new knowledge and what the philosopher Thomas Kuhn (1970) called a paradigm shift. Kuhn defined **paradigm** as "universally recognized scientific achievements that, for a time, provide model problems and solutions for a community of practitioners" (p. 10). A paradigm, he argued, is a world view that colors ideas and thoughts. For example, the world view in Europe during the European Middle Ages was that the world was flat. Christopher Columbus' journey helped to change that view and shift thinking towards a spherical earth although it was not readily accepted at first. Kuhn argued that paradigm shifts occur when anomalies cannot be explained by the existing paradigm and alternative theories and ideas are developed and debated, which creates a new paradigm. There are often disagreements between followers of the former and the new paradigm. As discussed above, the theory of gravity has undergone many revisions, which have resulted in paradigm shifts.

A paradigm shift occurred in the field of fashion scholarship during the middle of the 20th century. Prior, fashion was understood as a "trickle down" phenomenon (further explained in Chapter 3) where trends originated in the upper classes and were adopted by subsequently lower classes. However, in the 1960s a new phenomenon was observed, that the reverse was happening. This resulted in a reevaluation of the assumptions surrounding fashion knowledge and resulted in new theories. Additionally, more recently there has been a shift in the perception of clothing of traditional, non-western societies. It was often recited that fashion only existed in westernized societies and that non-western societies did not "have" fashion (e.g., Blumer, 1968; Flugel, 1930; Sapir, 1931; Simmel, 1904). It was argued that the appearance and dress of tribal and traditional cultures did not change but were static. However, the detailed study of traditional cultures has altered this perception (e.g., Cannon, 1998; Craik, 1994; Dalby, 1993; Dwyer, 2000; Jirousek; 1997; Nag, 1991; Niessen, 2007).

True theories should not be confused with lay theories. Lay theories are popular explanations for phenomena and have none to little evidentiary support but are believed to be factual. Hemline theory is a lay theory that is thought to link the height of women's skirt and dress hemlines to the economy. Some people believe the theory explains that when hemlines rise or fall the stock market will rise or fall. Other people believe that when the stock markets rises or falls so too will hemlines. Hemline theory is a lay theory that is often repeated by people who follow stock markets or follow fashion; however, its veracity and predictive validity is questionable. There is *some* evidence to corroborate a connection between stocks and hemlines but not enough to provide a definitive conclusion about the relationship (see Figure 1.2).

Hemlines have long been thought to be related to the stock market, an idea first proposed by economist George Taylor (Nystrom, 1928). He speculated that in good economic times women wore shorter skirts to reveal their silk stockings, which were a luxurious expense at the time; whereas in difficult economic times women wore longer skirts to hide the fact they were not wearing silk stockings. Researcher Mary Ann Mabry (1971) examined this theory and provided descriptive and statistical evidence of a relationship between the American stock market and hemlines. Mabry's overview of the decades reveals some preliminary data on the subject. In the 1900s and 1910s hemlines reached the ankle. In the 1920s, during a time of prosperity in the United States, hemlines moved from the ankle to the knee.

Figure 1.2 The connection between the stock market and hemlines is an example of a lay theory that has little to no evidentiary support but is commonly believed. Wavebreakmedia.

When the New York Stock Exchange crashed in 1929 and the world plummeted into a depression, hemlines fell to the mid-calf. World War II brought restrictions on fabric and goods but hemlines remained at the knee for the duration of the war. After the war, Christian Dior introduced a new silhouette which became known as the New Look. The 1950s were also a time of prosperity for the United States. Hemlines were below the knee and remained there until the mid-1950s. In 1957, Balenciaga introduced the sack dress which was designed with a higher hemline. The 1960s were also a time of prosperity and the mini-skirt was offered by Cardin, Courrèges and Mary Quant.

While descriptive evidence points to some possible support of this theory, Mabry (1971) further analyzed quantitative data for additional verification. She collected data from four fashion magazines and correlated the hemline length with data from the New York Stock Exchange from 1921 to 1971. She concluded that there is a positive relationship between hemline and stock market fluctuations. "Although there were several occasions when hemlines and stock market averages did not fluctuate hand-in-hand, enough indications were given to illustrate the similar movements of the two" (p. 66).

Mabry's research points to a statistical correlation between hemlines and the stock market. A correlation means two things happen at the same time, but does not mean there is necessarily a direct relationship. There may be a third variable that connects the two or it may just be coincidence. For example, imagine that you get headaches frequently and your doctor tells you to keep a record of when you get headaches. You do and notice that you get headaches on Mondays. You surmise that there is a connection or correlation between the two but this does not explain why you get headaches on a regular schedule. It may be that on Mondays you have a weekly lunch with a client and she wears perfume to which you are allergic. Or it may be that you are allergic to an ingredient in the food you eat at lunch. Or it may be that you are recovering from a wild weekend. Whatever the reason may be, there is an unknown variable that is causing the headaches. Likewise, there could be an unknown variable related to both stock markets and hemlines which has not yet been identified. Nonetheless, the connection has been repeated as evidence of a direct relationship among the population and treated as fact.

Economists Marjolein van Baardwijk and Philip Hans Franses further examined the connection between the stock market and hemlines for the time period 1921–2009. Their research yielded results that suggest a change in economic conditions precedes a change in hemlines by three years. Thus, they argue, a downtown in the economy will result in lower hemlines three years later. However, their methodology was highly dubious. They compared images in the French fashion magazines with economic data from the National Bureau of Economic Research that constituted a "world business cycle." Thus, while their statistical analysis might be accurate, their conclusions are likely based on faulty assumptions.

While this theory may have had some validity in the early 20th century, beginning in the 1960s the number of simultaneous fashion trends began to multiply. Today, any hemline length can be found in the market; Boho chic with long flowing skirts is found alongside super-short micro-skirts. Nonetheless, people continue to perpetrate the myth of a connection between hemlines and the stock market.

Why use theory?

So what is the point of theory and why do we need it or what can we do with it? The study of fashion helps us to understand how people interact and relate to each other. Clothing is a medium that represents genders, sexuality, race, ethnicity, class, psychology, society, culture, business, politics, philosophy, and so forth. By studying clothing and fashion we can interpret notions that have implications and impact on our daily lives, both locally and globally. Academic researchers of fashion and clothing strive to understand the way the world works and can use clothing as a lens to peer into other constructs. They use past and present phenomena to explain events and predict future styles, trends, actions, and behaviors related to clothing and fashion.

Researchers of fashion also can help current and future fashion professionals by interpreting their research findings into theories, models, frameworks, and constructs that have the potential to improve business professionals' goals. For most businesses the goals are to serve their clients in order to accrue a profit. While some business professionals may rely on their own intuition, their own experience, and formulate their own theories, models, frameworks, and constructs, academic findings can offer additional insight, different interpretations, and new venues for thought and action. For example, a retailer may have observed that fashion trends change from season to season in a linear direction, but without the understanding *why*, *how*, and *when* they will change, the retailer is left with only a partial understanding. All fashion professionals use—or should use—some degree of fashion forecasting in order to predict trends their clients will want. Most fashion professionals—designers, merchandisers, retailers, stylists, journalists, etc.—are not only working in the present to satisfy current client needs, but also planning to satisfy future needs. This takes a degree of research and insight; theories, models, frameworks, and constructs help to guide the decisions.

Accurate, validated theories are important to the field of fashion because they help guide decisions. As a burgeoning fashion professional, you will need to make decisions about products you wish to develop, buy, market, and sell in the future. Without sound reasoning (e.g., theory) your predictions of what will become a fashion are more likely to fail. For the fashion forecaster, the designer, or the merchandiser, this is a vital tool in planning, designing, manufacturing, and promoting collections. If you are able to predict that women will want higher hemlines over the next three years you have a better chance of designing saleable clothing. If you are able to predict that men will respond positively to the color mint green next spring you have a better chance of reaping profits and a better chance of becoming a leader in the fashion business. Predictions made on the basis of theory likely prove more accurate than predictions made on guesses or hunches.

Researchers in the sciences frequently investigate the relationship between independent variables and dependent variables. Independent variables are assumed to have an effect on dependent variables. That is, an independent variable can result in a change in the dependent variable by some connective means. Researchers make predictions about the relationship between two or more variables based on theory and develop hypotheses. The hypotheses are then tested. It will require many tests and different research studies to establish the validity of a theory.

In social scientific disciplines variables are studied using experiment, survey, observation, or interview. An experiment is commonly used in Psychology and is a manipulation whereby a condition of the independent variable is changed. The change can result in a change in the dependent variable. Experiment is the only way to deduce a causal relationship: A caused B because of C. For example, if you wanted to test if a new medicine (the independent variable) works on acne (the dependent variable), you would recruit a sample (participants) and divide them into two groups. One group would receive the acne medicine and one group would not (this is called the control group). If at the end of your experimental period, you observe that there is a difference in the level of acne in the group receiving the medicine you can surmise that the medicine caused the difference. If, however, you do not observe a difference in acne between the two groups at the end of the experimental period, you can surmise that the medicine had no influence.

A variation of an experiment can be to manipulate an original item, such as a photograph. For example, if you wanted to test if eye color affects perceptions of attractiveness, you could use duplicates of the same headshot of a person and change the eye color in each of the images. Because all else remains constant and only the eye color is altered, it is logical to assume that differences of perceived attractiveness are due to eye color. You then obtain a random sample of subjects (participants) and show them one of the images and ask them to rate the person's attractiveness on a scale. You continue this procedure and show many different people any of the images until all images have been reviewed and evaluated many times over (the number of times depends on your experimental design). After you collected all the data you analyze and find that a majority of your respondents find green eyes the most attractive. You can then surmise that a change in eye color causes a change in perceived attractiveness. Researcher R. Kelly Aune (1999) used an experiment to study how perfume affects perceptions of attractiveness and competence. Aune's method included participants being briefly interviewed by different people who were wearing differing amounts of perfume. When the interview was finished the interviewee evaluated the interviewer using a questionnaire. Aune analyzed the results to conclude that the amount of perfume an interviewer wore influenced perceived attractiveness and competence of the wearer.

Another method to test hypotheses is survey. Survey is common in Sociology and is used to generalize findings to the larger public when employed correctly. A survey involves collecting data via questionnaires. The questionnaires are frequently measures of a variable that have been tested and verified as accurate and reliable. After randomly-selected participants have completed your questionnaire, the data are analyzed using statistics. Statistical analysis can provide evidence of similarity/difference, correlation, or prediction. For example, if you wanted to find out if body image (independent variable) affects self-esteem (dependent variable) you would find effective and established scales of both variables, include them in a questionnaire, and give them to participants. Using statistical analysis you may find that a negative body image predicts low self-esteem, and conversely, that a positive body image predicts high self-esteem. Sophisticated statistical analyses such as structural equation modeling yield models that show pathways and connections between many variables. Researchers Alan C. Geller, Graham Colditz, Susan Oliveria, et al. (2002) employed the survey method to study tanning behaviors among children and adolescents. They gave questionnaires to more than 10,000 participants, then analyzed their responses using statistical procedures to identify sun protection attitudes and practices among their sample. Given the large sample size they had in their study they can make inferences based on their findings to the population at large.

Observation is also a method to record data. It is common in the field of Anthropology and is sometimes called field research or participant observation and involves the researcher seeing events or people in their natural environment. The researcher records their observations and interprets them to make conclusions. Participant observation often elicits information that the researcher would not obtain via survey or experiment because the participant may be unaware of the behavior or may not be truthful or accurate about it. For example, if you wanted to examine shopping behavior during a major sale you could go to a shopping mall and watch people. You may observe that people line up outside the store early the day of the sale, argue with other customers, and yell at sales people. In this method you may also interview or ask shoppers questions to understand their motivations or behavior. You could then surmise that a major sale affects customers' behavior. Fashion scholar Joanne Entwistle (2008) used this method to study masculinity among male models. She used interviews with models and bookers (the modeling agency's employee who books models) and sat in the offices of modeling agencies to observe models to evaluate and understand how male models negotiate their identity relative to gender and sexuality.

Researchers can also study behavior via examining history. Relationships between variables are assumed but not necessarily tested as in the case of experiment or survey. Historians often use primary and secondary sources to gather their information. Primary sources are original documents or artifacts, while secondary sources have already examined the primary sources and made conclusions or interpretations. For example, if you wanted to study the dress of cowboys in the 1880s, you could examine clothing that is preserved in museums and diaries written by cowboys (primary sources) as well as contemporary books and documentary films about cowboys. Historian Rachel K. Pannabecker (1996) used the historic method to study the incorporation of ribbon—a European product—into the authentic dress of the Great Lakes Native Americans. She used diaries, memorandums, accounting records, moccasins and other clothing items to examine the concept of cultural authentication (explained further in Chapter 4). A variation of this method was employed by fashion researcher Andrew Reilly (2008) to test Historic Continuity theory (explained in further detail in Chapter 2). Reilly used secondary sources—more than 2800 advertising images in magazines from 1900 to 1999—to evaluate how details of menswear evolve over time.

What is fashion?

Many people assume fashion is clothing, and although this may be true in a sense, fashion is actually much more complex and meaningful. Consider the following quotes about fashion:

- Fashion is "cultural technology that is purpose-built for specific locations" (Craik, 1994, p. xi).
- "Fashion, in a sense *is* change" (Wilson, 1985, p. 3) [italics original].
- Fashion is "a variation in an understood sequence, as a departure from the immediately preceding mode" (Sapir, 1931, p. 141).
- Fashion is "the eternal reoccurrence of the new" (Benjamin, 2003, p. 179).
- "Fashion is a general mechanism, logic or ideology that, among other things, applies to the area of clothing" (Svendsen, 2006, p. 12).
- "Fashion is a specific form of social change, independent of any particular object" (Lipovetsky, 1994, p. 16).
- "Fashion is not simply a change of styles of dress and adornment, but rather a systematic, structured and deliberate pattern of style change" (Polhemus, 2011, p.37).
- Fashion is "a prevailing custom, usage or style" (Merriam-Webster, 2013b, n.p.).

Based on these definitions, we can surmise the following: fashion is (a) an intangible force (b) that is manifested in tangible products, (c) that represent newness relative to prior fashion products, (d) are adopted by a group of people, and (e) are reflections of society and culture. Using this perspective, we can apply the concept of fashion to different products and industries.

In this text we need to distinguish between the terms clothing, dress, and fashion because these words are not interchangeable in fashion theory. *Clothing* is a product made out of a textile that is worn on the body; a shirt is an article of clothing. *Dress* includes three elements: (1) any item worn on the body (e.g., clothing, accessories); (2) any modification to the body (e.g., tanning, dieting, tattooing, hair styles); and (3) anything appended to the body (e.g., handbags, crutches, dog leashes, fans). A *fashion* is a form of dress or article of clothing that has or will become popular; bobbed hair was a fashion in the 1920s for women. *Fashion* is also a social process whereby an item of clothing or dress is adopted by many people; the fashion of the 1990s was influenced by music.

All dress is not fashion and fashion is not always dress. As discussed above, fashion is a process and can therefore be applied to industries beyond the clothing industry. The concept of fashion can be applied to any object or behavior or way of thinking. There is fashion in automobiles; in the late 1950s cars with fins were fashionable. There is fashion in the type of pets people own; in the 1920s it was fashionable to own German shepherds. There is even fashion in the type of social media used; MySpace fell out of fashion in favor of Facebook.

Specific to the fashion industry, the forces of popular acceptance influence areas other than clothing as well. Jewelry choices fluctuate with regard to gemstone, material, and design. Facial make-up and nail polish alter seasonably with changes to products, hues, application techniques, and overall aesthetics. Styles of shoes and belts wax and wane with specific details, as do lingerie, handbags, hosiery, hairstyles, fragrances, body shape, and body hair. And items like backpacks, skateboards, bikes, and electronic devices (e.g., smart phones and their covers) have become "fashion" items that are easily replaced.

Fashion is most often related to clothing because of the nature of the industry and its products. Forms of dress, such as apparel, jewelry, and accessories, are quicker to design, produce, and sell than other products. Automobiles take years from design to manufacture to popular acceptance and are costly to develop, produce, and buy. Furniture is expensive to manufacture, and replace or change frequently. Pets become beloved family members and people do not sell or replace them at whim for a new pet. But dress, being more affordable than other items such as cars or home interiors, is available to all people. In addition, dress is closer to the body making it more intimate and personal than one's choice in refrigerator color. And most everyone wears some form of dress, making it highly common. Thus, dress is a good source for the study of the process of fashion.

In westernized, capitalist societies, fashion as a process is a peculiar concept because products created as fashions are designed to have a short lifespan. They are designed to be popular for only a brief period of time. They are designed to die. This is known as **planned obsolescence** and it is the foundation of the western fashion system. If a trend does not end then there is no need to replace it. Fashions are created to sell in one season, have a brief and hopefully prosperous life, and then be discarded for something new.

The life of a fashion trend is viewed as a bell-curve, with the passage of time represented on the bottom and adoption represented on the left side (see Figure 1.3). At first, the item is adopted by a few people, but adoption increases with time until the market has been saturated and the item is at its most popular. Then adoption of the item declines until it eventually tapers out. A fashion trend is not to be confused with a fashion **fad** or **classic**. Fads are quick and sudden bursts of popularity and exist for a short period of time, such as calf-toning sneakers or feather extensions for hair in the early 2010s. Classics, in general, do not fluctuate in popularity and are found from season to season and year to year with little or no change. Examples of classic apparel items include Levi 501 jeans, khaki pants, and white t-shirts.

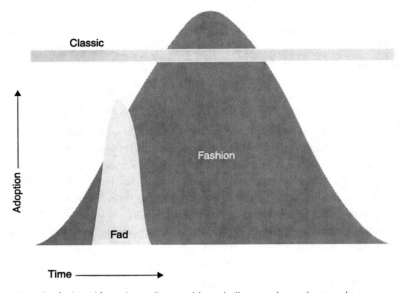

Figure 1.3 The fashion life-cycle as illustrated by a bell curve shows the introduction, acceptance, and decline of fashion, in relation to a fashion fad and a classic.

Who has fashion?

Fashion is often believed to be the domain of western culture, whereas clothing from other regions of the world was termed "ethnic" or "costume" or "traditional" in the erroneous belief that dress from other cultures did not change or follow trends; that is, other cultures were viewed as not having fashion. Fashion scholar Sandra Niessen (2007) argued that people were designated as without fashion as a means of categorizing us versus them, modern versus non-modern. Fashion from the western perspective was viewed as symptomatic of modernity, newness, and technology. Designating people as without fashion designated them as barbaric.[1] Contemporary researchers that argue that non-western societies have fashion trends are contrary to early fashion theorists who argued that fashion exists only in societies with social structure, where change is rapid, and "time" is acknowledged differently (e.g., Blumer, 1968; Flugel, 1930; Sapir, 1931; Simmel, 1904). Primitive cultures were thought to be "stuck" in time with little progress or adaption and thus provide a feeling of superiority for westerners. This perspective likely stems from research by early anthropologists who visited tribal cultures for limited amounts of time and were not there long enough to witness change as defined by western standards (Niessen, 2007).

Likewise, fashion scholar Jennifer Craik (1994) also argued that the ethnocentric view of fashion as a Euro/American phenomenon is inaccurate. She argued that the idea that non-western people have static modes of dress is incorrect. Craik (2009) noted that the Chola women of La Paz, Bolivia have a distinctive type of dress that is both customary and fashionable. The skirts they wear are called polleras and women usually wear multiple polleras at one time. Each year new styles of pollera in new fabrics and decorative appliques are offered, thus creating a fashion cycle where old styles are abandoned and new styles adopted. Craik (1994) similarly argued that fashion exists among the Mount Hagen residents of Papua New Guinea. During an annual festival, tribal members gather for a celebration and adorn themselves with unique headdresses, made of such varied materials as feathers, bones, flowers, birds, fauna, fur, teeth, and human hair. The materials are combined to create unique looks that are a combination of traditional aesthetics and individual preference. "There is no doubt that such radiant displays are not just the uniform of custom but exhibit individual interpretations, innovations, and adaptions" (Craik, 2009, p. 55). Thus, Craik argued, fashion also exists in this traditional community.

Ethno-historian Charlotte Jirousek (1997) questioned the difference between fashion and traditional dress as well and examined the clothing changes among men in the Turkish village of Çömlekçi. Western forms of dress were first introduced by the late 19th century. In the 1920s, Western dress forms were originally intended by the governing bodies to "modernize" the people of Turkey, but the residents of Çömlekçi, rather, appropriated the new forms and made them part of their culture. In 1964, although village men wore western clothing, "the mode of dress remained essential traditional, in spite of outward appearance of modernization" (p. 208). Tailored slacks were accompanied by white, long-sleeve shirts (buttoned to the collar by older men and unbuttoned by younger men) along with hand-knitted sweater vests, over which suit jackets were worn. A brimless hat, such as a golf cap or a skullcap was worn (the hat needed to be brimless to align with religious dictates that the head must be covered during prayer and the wearer must touch his head to the ground during prayer), though some men wore fedoras. Frequently, a musket was carried as an accessory. A village tailor made the clothing but by the 1960s ready-to-wear shirts were available. By the 1980s, villagers were exposed to different forms of dress through television and the tourists who visited the village. By the 1990s, there was a multiplicity of dress mass-manufactured dress styles, including jeans, tank tops, t-shirts, shorts, sweaters, and suit jacket, worn mostly by the younger generation. The older generation continued to wear their traditional clothing.

Jirousek (1997) argued that as Turkey sought to reform and modernize at the beginning of the 20th century, "a set of European fashion system garments was adopted into a traditional dress system and continued in the initial form, essentially without further change, throughout much of [the 20th] century . . . The superficial appearance of westernization of dress in fact does not justify the assumption that the wearer is westernized" (p. 212). Thus, the garments had become culturally authenticated (see Chapter 4), but they were still in a traditional dress system. The system began to change to a mass-fashion system with the arrival of electricity, television, tourists, and later by the introduction of mass-produced fabrics and ready-to-wear clothing. By the mid-1990s, Jirousek asserts the transition to a mass-fashion system was virtually complete; older village men wore their traditional suits in the village but changed to a fashionable look when going to town, while the younger men wore fashionable attire regardless of location.

In addition to the above, fashion has been noted in garments that have typically been described as static: the sari of India (Dwyer, 2000), the sari of Bengal (Nag, 1991), the dress of Canadian Native peoples (Cannon, 1998), the kimono of Japan (Dalby, 1993), and the dress of China during the Ming period (Brook, 1999). Thus, while the western fashions system may be the most discussed in texts and literature, and probably the best known given globalization, other systems of fashion exist. Contrary to popular assumption and belief, fashion exists outside of industrial societies as well. Although this book is intended for students who likely will work in a western-styled fashion system, examples of fashion from non-western or non-industrialized societies will also be discussed.

Fashioning the body

In the same vein that fabric has been cut, folded, manipulated, and decorated to create aesthetic effects so too has the body been cut, folded, manipulated, and decorated. One of the most common body fashions is to reshape its silhouette using undergarments. The corset is one of the early inventions that helped women achieve a fashionable figure, be it an hourglass shape of slim waist with curved bust and hips or a slim silhouette that compressed the bust and hips into a tubular shape. Historically, corsets were made of fabric that was stiffened with animal bones, metal or plastic. Laces in the front or back were used to tighten areas in order to reshape the body. Women were not alone in wearing corsets; men too were fond of what the corset could do to one's figure and these were especially prominent on men's bodies in the early 19th century. Although corsets may have fallen out of fashion, other silhouette-modifying creations, such as girdles, brassieres, and high-compression underwear and shirts, helped men and women achieve the desired silhouette. For example, the pannier, popular in 18th century Europe, emphasized a woman's hips (see Figure 1.4).

Decorating the body with tattoos is another example of fashion. Whereas tattoos were once reserved for tribal cultures, avant-garde artists, and criminals, by the 1990s they were becoming fashionable in Europe and American societies. Although some people may argue that tattoos cannot be fashion because of their permanence (Polhemus, 1994; Curry, 1993), dress scholar Llewellyn Negrin (2008) argues that tattoos have become fashionable and notes different styles of tattoos are fashionable at different times. Negrin wrote:

> [A]lthough the physically permanent nature of tattoos may seem to mitigate against their use as fashion icons, their semiotic multivalency led to their widespread employment in the marketing of men's styles. Whereas tattoos are often used by individuals in a bid to fix their identity by permanently imprinting it onto their skin, it is their very *un*-fixity of meaning that has led to their appropriation by the fashion and advertising industries. (pp. 334–335)

Figure 1.4 The silhouette of the body has been modified through history to achieve different silhouettes. This panier and corset from the 18th century illustrate one such fashionable outline. Victoria and Albert Museum, London.

Another way the body can be aesthetically altered is by tanning or bleaching. Tanning darkens the skin tone while bleaching lightens the skin. Tanning can be done naturally by exposing the skin to the sun's rays, or artificially by exposing the skin to ultraviolet light or by applying creams and sprays that can cosmetically darken the skin. Bleaching can be achieved by applying creams or dermatological products to the skin. People of all races, geographic locations, and classes participate in tanning or bleaching and the reasons vary (Christopher, 2012). Some people like the aesthetic of darkened or lightened skin because it is fashionable, some use darkened or lightened skin as a way to signal status (e.g., people who work in fields are tanned, so lighter skin symbolizes a life of luxury indoors; lighter skin symbolizes people who work indoors, so darker skin symbolizes lounging on the beach); and still others view it as a way to differentiate one group of people from another.

Other ways the body has been altered for fashionable purposes include branding, piercing, hair removal, hair extension, breast enlargement, liposuction, circumcision, dieting, slenderizing undergarments, protein shakes, working out, and body building. In all these examples it was the body that was transformed, thus making it a vital component in the examination of dress and fashion change.

Put a pot of water on the stove and turn the burner on high heat. Watch it. It will take a few minutes to start to see some activity but eventually you will see little bubbles—like champagne bubbles—start to form. There will not be many at first but more will develop and then they will get larger. Soon there will be big bubbles, but the entire pot will not be boiling until one specific moment when suddenly—*wham!*—the entire pot of water is boiling. Malcolm Gladwell (2002) termed this the "**tipping point.**" It is the point at which nothing becomes something.

Gladwell argued that fashion trends can be thought of as epidemics; rather than the element studied being a contagion, the element is contagious behavior. He argued there are similarities in the way a disease and a fashion trend spread. The tipping point is when a trend gets noticed. He identified three rules:

1. The **Law of the Few**. Some people have more influence than others. These people are **connectors, mavens**, and **salespeople**. *Connectors* know lots of people and connect disparate groups. They transfer information or knowledge from one group to another. *Mavens* have the ability to start epidemics by talking. They are well-informed and are viewed as sources of information. Gladwell likened them to "information brokers" who use word-of-mouth to pass along interesting or important information. Their aim is not personal gain but simply to help people. *Salespeople* are critical to the epidemic because they are the ones who can persuade others to take action. They are at the cusp of the tipping point.
2. The **Stickiness Factor**. Messages need to be "sticky." There needs to be something memorable about the information. In fashion a new design or way of styling needs to be memorable. Sometimes this comes in the garment itself, in the way it is styled, or in the way it is presented in promotions.
3. The **Power of Context**. Epidemics are sensitive to context. They are dependent on the environment as to whether they will spread or die. Gladwell wrote, "an epidemic can be reversed, can be tipped, by tinkering with the smallest details of the immediate environment" (p. 146).

Gladwell cites Hushpuppy shoes to illustrate his concept. By 1994 Hushpuppy shoes were hopelessly out of fashion after rampant success in the 1950s and 1960s, and the company was about to close. Perhaps for the fact they were so out-of-date that some chic youths in the East Village of New York City began to buy them at vintage stores. Those youths were noticed by others who also began buying Hushpuppy shoes at vintage stores too. Soon designers such as Isaac Mizrahi, John Bartlett, and Anna Sui incorporated Hushpuppy shoes into their collections, resulting in the shoes and company being revived from the brink of extinction and the iconic shoes becoming fashionable again. In this case, the youth who began wearing the vintage shoes again were a few of the connectors, those that followed their example were mavens, and fashion designers were salespeople. The message was particularly sticky; they were so out of fashion they had to be noticed. The context was that the fashion culture was fascinated with vintage clothing and ironic, retro looks. By 1995 the interest in Hushpuppy shoes had tipped and became a legitimate trend.

Semiotics

Semiotics is the study of signs and sign systems. Anything can be a sign and represent an idea or concept; a heart can represent love, a gold band on a finger can represent marriage, an olive branch can represent peace. Linguist Ferdinand de Saussure (1966) argued that a sign is made of a signified and a signifier; the ***signifier*** is a sound-image while the ***signified*** is what it represents. For our purposes we will extend the sound-image to include visual objects. The connection between signifier and signified is governed by a **code**. For example, the color of a cowboy's hat in Western movies is coded. The hat is the signifier and its meaning is the signified. In classic Western movies, the cowboys in white hats (the signifier) are considered good (the signified), whereas cowboys in black hats (the signifier) are typically bad (the signified). This coding creates a short-hand for the observer; without knowing anything about a character the viewer can immediately recognize the heroes from the villains.

In general, all dress can be considered semiotic because all dress is embedded with meaning; however, people can interpret the specific meaning differently because codes are a product of enculturation and socialization. A fur coat can mean different things to different people. It can mean warmth and protection from snow; it can mean luxury and status; it can mean death and cruelty. One's history as an Eskimo, fashionista, or animal-rights activist colors the way in which the fur is interpreted. See Figure 1.5.

Modern, postmodern, post-postmodern

In the past century the world has transitioned from the "**modern**" era to the "**postmodern**" era in what can be considered a paradigm shift. Modernism is the belief in rationalism and universal truth. Those who subscribe to modern thought believe in tradition and that there is only one correct way to do something. Postmodernism is a reaction to modernism. Rather than accepting traditions as a universal truth, the postmodern perspective questions them. For example, a modern painting depicts people in a realistic way, but a postmodern painting might depict the same people but in a rendering that is highly stylized, such as the comic-strip style in Roy Lichtenstein's *Reverie* (see Figure 1.6). A modern sculpture might depict a bust of a famous person, but a postmodern artist might depict a famous word, such as Robert Indiana's LOVE sculpture where the letters of the word are the sculpture. A modern film might show the beginning, middle, and end of a story in that order, but a postmodern film might reverse or jumble the order; in *Memento* the first scene of the film is the last scene of the story and the film is shown in reverse; in *Pulp Fiction* the first scene begins in the middle of the story.

When we look at dress we can see differences between modern and postmodern perspectives. From a modern perspective there are expected rules to follow: do not wear white shoes after Labor Day[2]; do not wear plaid with polka-dots; do not wear

Figure 1.5 This cartoon lampoons the semiotic nature of dress; nonetheless it illustrates varied signifiers and signifieds of clothing. Roz Chast/The New Yorker Collection/www.cartoonbank.com.

pajamas to school. From a postmodern perspective these rules are challenged, disrupted, and violated: white is worn after Labor Day, violating a long-standing rule of fashion; plaid and polka-dots are combined to provide a new aesthetic experience; pajamas are worn to school, challenging social conventions.

Dress scholar Marcia Morgado (1996) noted that rejection of authority is central to postmodern philosophy. By virtue of rejecting authority, **questioning** begins. Questioning is challenging the traditional, acceptable modes of dress (Damhorst, 2005) such as wearing white shoes after Labor Day. In the modern era rules dictated

Figure 1.6 *Reverie* by Roy Lichtenstein exemplifies postmodernism in its unusual and challenging approach to painting. Estate of Roy Lichtenstein.

what styles of dress were acceptable to wear based on one's status, age, occupation, and gender. But in the postmodern era the rules are disrupted to create unique, individual compositions; a wedding dress could be worn with combat boots or expensive diamond jewelry could be worn with sweatpants. Sometimes you might hear the term *mixing* used synonymously with questioning, such as creating a multi-cultural aesthetic by mixing different dress items from different ethnic communities. Questioning can also lead to *irony*, another element that is typical of postmodern fashion. For example, modern fashion would have rules against adults accessorizing with children's toys but in the postmodern era the irony of an adult wearing jewelry made of children's toys is appreciated (see Figure 1.7).

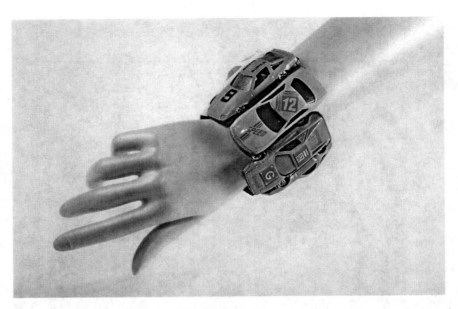

Figure 1.7 This bracelet, made from children's Matchbox cars, represents the ironic element of postmodernism in dress. Bracelet courtesy of Lori Yancura; image by Attila Pohlmann.

Another form of questioning is the use of *androgyny*. Androgyny comes from a Greek word meaning "man and woman" and hence androgyny is the blending together of masculinity and femininity. It should not be confused with unisex which is the absence of masculinity and femininity. Overalls are unisex but not necessarily androgynous. There are a number of ways that androgyny can be incorporated into fashion: feminine fabrics, such as lace, could be pared with masculine fabrics, such as leather; a tailored men's jacket could be paired with a flowing skirt; a man with masculine facial features can sport soft, flowing curls of hair, or a woman with curved, delicate facial features can sport short, cropped hair. Postmodernism is a reaction to modernism's rules, so androgyny challenges modernist conventions of femininity and masculinity by violating the rules by *mixing* them. The punk, goth, and grunge subcultures and the subsequent trends they inspired contained androgynous elements. Additionally, models like Erika Linder, and Harmony Boucher, and Andrej Pejic exemplify the androgynous aesthetic and are frequently hired for men's and women's fashion shows and advertisements.

Another important element of postmodern fashion is valuing an item for its aesthetics rather than its symbolic meaning (Morgado, 1996). Wearing a crucifix or rosary or Star of David around one's neck would be considered postmodern if the wearer wears it because it is "cool" or "stylish" rather than because it symbolizes a religious conviction. In the Jewish faith a Kabbalah bracelet is a red string tied around the left wrist and is linked to ancient, mystical teachings. It is believed to protect the wearer from harm. The Kabbalah bracelet became a fashion statement for many in the 2000s after celebrities like Madonna embraced the faith and adopted the bracelet. Followers of celebrity culture adopted the red bracelet with little understanding of its meaning, but rather liked the look. Another instance of placing aesthetics over symbolism is when people adopted "tribal" tattoos as fashion without understanding the cultural significance of the design. Often, tribal tattoos carry meaning with them such as achieving adulthood or accomplishing a goal and are frequently sacred. When people began adopting "cool designs" for their body art they were practicing postmodern fashion.

Scholars have also noted that we appear to be entering into a new phase and have used many different labels to call this new era, including altermodermism (Bourriaud, 2009), hypermodernity (Lipovetsky, 2005), performatism (Eschelman, 2000, 2001), automodernity (Samuels, 2008), digimodernism (Kirby, 2009), and metamodernism (Vermeulen & van den Akker, 2010). Morgado (in press) analyzed five of the prevailing concepts, used the popular term **"post-postmodernism"** as an umbrella term, and identified elements of the new era relevant to fashion and dress. She surmised the following: post-postmodernist dress includes new designs that are the result of collaboration between business (e.g., the retail store or brand) and consumers; excessive consumption for the pleasure of consumption but mixed with anxiety about personal impact on the environment and anxiety about personal debt; styles that utilize cyber technology; random mixture of aesthetic elements and principles, and infantile or childish styles for adults. Examples of post-postmodern dress include *NIKEiD* from Nike where consumers can select styles, colors, and patterns to create a custom-designed shoe; shopping for fast fashion[3] items that one will wear only a few times before discarding them while anxious about the impact this will have on the environment and personal debt; cyberpunk and steampunk styles that blend technology with fashionable components; and Hello Kitty accessories for adults. However, Morgado noted that other than cyberpunk and steampunk, these fashion examples can also be explained by postmodernism, and therefore if we are entering a new era we are at the cusp of it and have not seen post-postmodernism's full impact on fashion as of yet.

Organization of text

In academia, fashion has often been considered the inferior relative to the more established disciplines of engineering, mathematics, chemistry, physiology, psychology, sociology, and anthropology. Many people consider fashion frivolous. It is considered unnecessary. It is considered unworthy of serious attention. This is because fashion has long been considered to be the domain of women and therefore silly. Indeed, men are often thought to "not have fashion" and when they do they are European, and if not European, they are black, Asian, Latino, or a race other than white, and if they are white, they are gay, and if they are not gay but straight, they are an oddity. But a cultural shift in the 1990s began to look at fashion differently. Museums and documentaries explained the deeper meaning and significance of fashion and universities were offering rigorous programs in fashion theory. While the perception of fashion has changed somewhat, there is still considerable distance between "respectable" disciplines and fashion curriculums.

Two academic traditions exist in the study of fashion, although there is overlap between them at times: Fashion Studies and Clothing and Textiles. Fashion Studies came from established disciplines such as art, art history, humanities, and museum curation. These disciplines were respected fields, although the study of fashion tended to be marginalized. However, in the 21st century, Fashion Studies programs started to form that examined fashion from a unified perspective. Meanwhile, the Clothing and Textiles perspective originated in Home Economics departments in the United States. Beginning in the 1850s, young men were educated in agricultural programs, whereas young women were educated in cooking, household maintenance, child rearing, and sewing. The Clothing and Textiles discipline grew out of the sewing curriculum. In the 1960s, the discipline shifted from matters of the home to matters of industry, and branched into merchandising, marketing, retail management, textiles, history and social-psychology of dress and appearance. Fashion scholar Erfat Tseëlon (2012) categorized those who study fashion into two different groups: fashion natives and fashion migrants. Fashion natives work with artifacts of dress to "chronicle, classify, categorize [and] describe uses" (p. 4), whereas fashion migrants come from social science fields and examine abstract ideas related to dress, such "meanings, functions, [and] reasons" of dress (p. 4). Today, generally, Fashion Studies programs focus on critique, analysis, and interpretation of meanings of fashion, whereas Clothing and Textiles programs examine industry components, although there is overlap among some scholars and researchers in the field. In this text, examples from both perspectives are included.

The sections of this text are organized based on a continuum developed by fashion scholar Jean Hamilton (1997). Hamilton argued that fashion occurs at two levels: at the micro, or individual level, and at the macro, or group level. Spanning these levels are four systems that each contribute to the process of fashion: individual, social, cultural and the fashion system.

In Chapter 1 you were introduced to theory and basic terms and concepts. In Chapter 2 you will read about the individual influence to understand the role unique people have in the fashion process. In Chapter 3 you will read about social influence to understand how groups of people innovate and react to fashions. In Chapter 4 you will read about culture to understand what types of cultures support and do not support fashion systems. In Chapter 5 you will read about the fashion system to understand the business of fashion. And finally Chapter 6 will include examples of fashion failures and conclude the book. After completing this text you will have a good foundation for understanding how, where, why, and when fashion exists.

BOXED CASE 1.1. RUDD/LENNON MODEL OF BODY AESTHETICS

Creating a visual appearance is more complex than one would think. The act of dressing appears to be simply putting on clothes, but underneath this straightforward behavior lay a constellation of variables that influence our dress selections. The Rudd/Lennon model of body aesthetics helps us to understand these influences (Reilly & Rudd, 2009, p. 236; see Figure 1.8). Cultural, social, and psychological variables influence the aesthetic creation. That creation (i.e., the visual appearance) is pre-tested and feedback is gathered from other people. Based on this feedback you do nothing, you change your appearance, you change your personal standard of what you consider attractive, or you try to change the cultural standard of what is considered attractive. This model can be used to understand how and why people dress themselves.

For example, if you were dressing for a job interview you would start by selecting your apparel based on the cultural ideal which leads to the box marked "created appearance." The cultural ideal for a job interview is conservative dress in muted or dark colors. Your selection is influenced by comparing yourself with others and anxiety. You decide to wear a suit made of navy pinstripe wool and paired with a matching white and blue stripe shirt

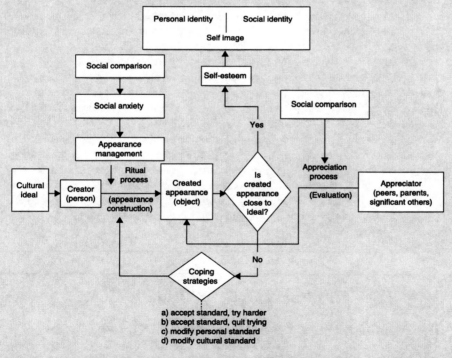

Figure 1.8 The Rudd/Lennon model of body aesthetics illustrates the complete system of creating a personal aesthetic. International Textile and Apparel Association/Sage.

25

and red tie. You receive feedback from your roommate and mother; your roommate says "I don't like it" and your mother says "That's an odd shirt to wear—the pattern is too busy." You realize at this point that your best option is to change your shirt into a plain white one (thus, you accepted a standard and are trying harder to achieve it). Wearing your new shirt, you receive additional feedback from your roommate ("You look good") and your mother ("That's better") and you are ready for your interview.

As you examine the model consider your own style of dressing—which path did you take?

BOXED CASE 1.2. MASLOW'S HIERARCHY AND FASHION

Some cultures or organizations have strict rules as to what people can and cannot wear—such as dress codes enforced by businesses, schools, fraternities, or sororities[4] (belonging). Some groups of people may not have strict rules about what to wear but have a certain look that identifies them, such as punks or motorcycle clubs or cowboys; in order to belong one must dress like them (love/belonging). Some people choose items of dress because it makes them feel good about themselves or gives them status (esteem), such as wearing gold. Some individuals may want to express their individuality and potential by creating appearances that reflect their inner-being (actualization).

People wear fashion for reasons different from wearing clothing. One way to understand the different motivations that people have for wearing clothing versus fashion is to use a model developed by psychologist Abraham Maslow (1943). Maslow developed a hierarchy of needs and postulated that people pass through a series of stages to meet their needs. According to Maslow, the first need is physiological, the second need is safety, the third need is belonging, the fourth need is esteem, and the final need is self-actualization. If we take this concept and apply it to dress, we can see that dress can satisfy the need for safety, such as keeping you warm or dry or protected from insects. But as people strive to belong to groups and to feel good about themselves, the role of dress can shift from clothing to fashion. Maslow's hierarchy is a good way to organize dress and analyze different motives. It can be a useful tool for professionals in fashion, advertising, promotion, and image-consulting.

BOXED CASE 1.3. FASHION IS A MEME

A **meme** is an idea or style that is replicated and spread among people. Slogans can be a meme, like "Have a Coke and a Smile" or McDonald's "I'm lovin' it," or Nike's "Just do it!" Quotes can be meme, like "Life is like a box of chocolates" from *Forest Gump* (1994) or "Frankly, my dear, I don't give a damn!" from *Gone with the Wind* (1939) or "This ain't my first time at the rodeo" from *Mommie Dearest* (1981). Memes can also be more complex, like conspiracy theories, fairy tales, or behavior (such as tapping the breast twice followed by flashing a peace sign.) They become part of the popular culture and are passed from person to person very quickly in different formats. These quotes or ideas have been replicated on t-shirts, mugs, bumper stickers, refrigerator magnets, lapel pins, texts, email addresses, decorative plates, television shows, songs, jokes and more.

You read about Gladwell's concept of the tipping point—that fashion can be like a contagion or virus that spreads rapidly. His idea is similar to that of a meme. It is passed from person to person, in different forms, rapidly. It is replicated and spreads out like a virus. Fashion can spread from person to person, neighborhood to neighborhood, from city to city, from region to region, and can theoretically and metaphorically be contagious.

Summary

Fashion is a process whereby an item—such as a form of clothing or dress—becomes popularized during a specific period of time. Fashion is accepted first by a few people and grows in acceptance with time until it has reached a saturation point, and then it declines in popularity. Fashion should not be confused with clothing. Not all fashion is clothing, and not all clothing is fashion; some clothing does not conform to the "rules" of fashion and some items that are not even dress-related are fashionable.

Fashion theory attempts to explain why some items become popular while other items do not. Fashion theory is studied by academics and industry professionals to explain personality, social movements, cultural ideals, business practices. It is hoped that, with accurate theories of fashion, business can make informed decisions about what to create, produce, sell, and market. Theories, ideas, and concepts are created to explain fashion. Some theories, ideas, and concepts are validated while others have been modified. New theories or modifications to existing theories are often the result of a paradigm shift. Like clothing trends, fashion theories can also become fashionable themselves in their popularity and use.

Key Terms

- Classic
- Clothing
- Code
- Concept
- Conceptual framework
- Connectors
- Dress
- Fad
- Fashion
- Hypothesis

- Law
- Law of the few
- Mavens
- Meme
- Modern
- Paradigm
- Planned obsolescence
- Postmodern
- Post-postmodern
- Power of context

- Questioning
- Salespeople
- Semiotics
- Signified
- Signifier
- Stickiness factor

- Taxonomy
- Theory
- Theoretical framework
- Tipping point
- Trend

Discussion questions

1. When do you think a trend becomes noticed? When do you notice a trend?
2. Is your mode of dress modern, postmodern, or post-postmodern?
3. According to Gladwell there are three groups of people important to fashion: connectors, mavens, and sales people. Which are you?
4. Name different types of questioning you have noticed in people's modes of dress. Which of these were aesthetic and which were symbolic?

Learning activities

1. Create a taxonomy to categorize the clothing items found in your wardrobe. Examples of categories can be: fiber (natural, manufactured, mixed), country where made, design (solid, stripe, or patterned), color, style (casual, professional, special occasion), etc. After you have completed your inventory, do you see any gaps or areas where you have more of one category than others?
2. Collect images of fashion items and categorize them as modern, postmodern, or post-postmodern. Identify their characteristics. How would you redesign one of the modern items to make it postmodern, or post-postmodern?
3. Collect advertisements of dress and group into two groups: clothing and fashion. Within each group, arrange the advertisements according to Maslow's hierarchy of needs. How do the groupings compare? Does clothing have more images in one level than fashion? Why do you think advertisers choose to market products differently and how do you think consumers react to these different marketing strategies?
4. Bring in an item of dress from your closet and discuss with the class its semiotic elements. What are the signifiers and signifieds? Are there any elements that might be misinterpreted or read differently by other people?

Notes

1. Indeed, fashion historian Valerie Steele (1998) has noted the myth of Parisian fashion as superior to other fashions by designating as barbaric non-Parisians who did not dress as well as Parisians.
2. Labor Day is an American holiday celebrated in the beginning of each September. It is frequently considered to be the beginning of the Fall season. With regard to fashion, white shoes are considered

summer shoes and worn between Memorial Day in May (the start of the summer season) and Labor Day. Likewise, alcoholic drinks followed a similar cycle; clear alcohol (e.g., vodka) in summer, dark alcohol (e.g., rum) in winter.

3. Fast fashion is a retail concept where inexpensive trendy clothing is produced and sold quickly. The fact that the clothing is poorly made is negated by the fact that it is inexpensive and can be replaced easily.

4. Fraternities and sororities are social organizations at many colleges in the United States. Potential members, or pledges, apply to become members and undergo a period of initiation before they are accepted.

Further reading

Bovone, L. (2006). Urban style cultures and urban cultural production in Milan: Postmodern identity and the transformation of fashion. *Poetics, 34* (6), 370–382.

Goldsmith, R. E., Flynn, L. R., & Moore, M. A. (1996). The self-concept of fashion leaders. *Clothing and Textiles Research Journal, 14* (4), 242–248.

Gordon, B. (2009). American denim: Blue jeans and their multiple layers of meaning. In P. McNeil and V. Karaminas (eds) *The Men's Fashion Reader* (331–340). Oxford: Berg.

Hagen, K. (2008). Irony and ambivalence: Postmodernist issues in the fashion world. In P. Giuntini & K. Hagen (eds) *Garb: A Fashion and Culture Reader* (pp. 101–110). Upper Saddle River, New Jersey: Pearson Education, Inc.

Holloman, L. O. (1991). Black sororities and fraternities: A case study in clothing symbolism. In Patricia A. Cunningham & Susan Voso Lab (eds) *Dress and Popular Culture* (pp. 46–60). Bowling Green, Ohio: Bowling Green State University Popular Press.

Reilly, A., & Rudd, N. A. (2009). Social anxiety as predictor of personal aesthetic among women. *Clothing and Textiles Research Journal, 27* (3), 227–239.

2

FASHION AND THE INDIVIDUAL

Uniqueness is an important concept in initiating and propelling fashion trends. Some people do not want to dress like others. Some people want to be different—to show they do not follow social conventions, are individualistic, or are artistic—and to do this they purposefully avoid wearing the current fashions or trends. What is considered unique can be something that is similar to the current trend but slightly different. If wide collars are in vogue they might wear a very wide collar, thus advancing a fashion trend (see "Historic Continuity theory", this chapter p. 45). Or what is considered unique can be something completely different, like wearing silver jewelry when gold jewelry is the trend.

The body is also a site for people to exhibit uniqueness and in doing so have instigated new fashion trends. In the middle of the 20th century, in Europe and the United States, having a tattoo made a person unique, but by the end of the century singular tattoos were common. People who desired a different look found new ways to aesthetically alter their skin. Singular tattoos were followed by numerous tattoos and sleeves (see irezumi in Chapter 4) and glow-in-the-dark tattoos. Likewise, pierced ear lobes had become commonplace, so people who desired uniqueness turned to piercing ear cartilage, eyebrows, navels, nipples, wrists and necks. By the 21st century, a new trend had emerged—medical-grade metal pieces were implanted under the skin to give a new dimension to the body and ear plugs were stretching the earlobe to new proportions. These changes demonstrated how something once considered unique, once popularized, needs to be replaced with a new concept or form.

Fashion is often a curious dance between two opposing forces—the desire to fit in and the desire to be different. As a concept *uniqueness* helps us to understand why some fashions die and some new ones begin. Some people—like fashion innovators and fashion leaders—do not want to wear what everyone else is wearing. When a market becomes saturated with a style they strive to find something different, and by doing so sometimes launch a new trend. The desire to not follow the fashion trends—or anti-fashion—is also a strong influence on many people's choice of dress. They may feel fashion is frivolous or consumerist and purposefully wear clothing that is not in fashion, but ironically what is not in fashion at this particular moment can be alluring to others, who then adopt it and disseminate it to others, thereby continuing the fashion life-cycle.

Fashion innovators and fashion leaders are individuals who create new styles or communicate a new style early in its life-cycle (see Figure 2.1). By virtue of being seen in the new style or telling others about it, they help to instigate a new trend. Similarly, an individual can kill a trend by declaring it dead. For example, celebrities

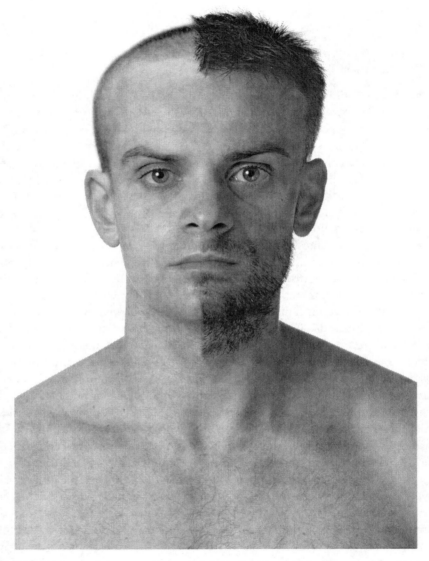

Figure 2.1 Unique styles can ignite a trend if they are copied by other people who value difference. Vladyslav Starozhylov/Shutterstock.com.

such as actress Katharine Hepburn, actress Catherine Deneuve, actress Catherine Zeta Jones, the Duchess of Cambridge Katherine Windsor, model Kate Moss, and singer Katy Perry have influenced fashion greatly. Yet, one does not need to be an international celebrity to influence fashion; average consumers do it every day in what they choose and do not choose to purchase.

The fashion curve presented in Chapter 1 aligns with the type of person who adopts a trend. In the beginning, fashion leaders are the first group of people to adopt the trend (Rogers, 1962). **Fashion innovators** are people who take a chance with wearing something new or unique, be it a new product or a new way of wearing an existing product. Often this can be a celebrity or a well-known person or someone who is considered an authority on fashion. This person is seen wearing the style which in turn disseminates it to other people, such as fashion communicators. **Fashion communicators** are viewed as authorities on fashion and help to popularize the growing trend by wearing it and talking about it. For example, the style might be mentioned in a magazine or seen on a television show or at a red carpet event. Note the similarities between these terms and Gladwell's terms of mavens and salespeople (as discussed in Chapter 1). Next, the population majority and population minority adopt the item, followed by fashion laggards until finally the trend expires. This system of communicating fashion trends from one group to another is known as the **adoption and diffusion model** (Rogers, 1962).

This chapter examines how the individual interacts with fashion. The Public, Private, and Secret Self model is presented first in order to understand people's different levels of expression. The model posits that people dress to reveal different facets of their life—from the public self that anyone can see to the secret self that is hidden from others. This theory is followed by the concept of body image—the way a person perceives their body and what they do about their body affects how they dress it or the methods he or she may take to change it. Body image is a significant issue in fashion right now as the fashion industry is criticized for creating unrealistic body standards that affect people negatively. Aesthetic Perception and Learning theory explains that people need to learn to understand or appreciate a new design or style of dressing in order to accept it. Two theories are presented that touch upon the role of boredom in fashion change. When people become bored with a style they look for a new way to dress, as explained by the theories of shifting erogenous zones and historic continuity. Lastly, Symbolic Interaction theory explains how the individual interacts with society in order to create meaning.

The Public, Private, and Secret Self

The **Public, Private, and Secret Self model** is a taxonomy for categorizing different types of dress at different levels of expression. The model was originally proposed by dress scholar Joanne Eicher (1981) who based her work on research developed by sociologist Gregory Stone (1965). Stone argued that two categories of dress exist: reality and fantasy. Reality dressing, or anticipatory socialization as he termed it, is dressing for a realistic job you hope to hold one day—such as wearing a business suit in the hopes of working for a bank. Fantastic socialization, however, is dressing for a job that is not realistic, but imaginary, like dressing as a Stormtrooper from *Star Wars*. Eicher (1981) furthered this idea and divided dress into public, private, and secret levels. It was later expanded by Eicher and Miller (1994).

The taxonomy divides dress into three types (reality, fun/leisure, and fantasy). Reality dress is realistic attire that may be related to one's gender, work, or hobbies. Fun/leisure dress is worn outside of work situations and may be dress for dating, exercise, or sporting evenings. Fantasy dress is escapist and may include costumes and sexual fantasies. These three categories are crossed with three aspects of the self (public, private, and secret). The public self is the part of us that anyone can see, and usually includes clothing we wear to work, run errands, or in professional situations. The private self is revealed to friends and family but is likely not seen by the general public. The secret self is hidden from others or may be revealed only to intimates. According to the taxonomy, the level of self interacts with the type of dress to create nine distinct cells: public × reality, public × fun/leisure, public × fantasy, etc. This grid helps to analyze situations related to dress (see Table 2.1).

Institutions, such as workplaces, governments, and religions often administer rules for dressing the public self. Businesses determine dress codes, such as jacket and tie for banking professions or uniforms for police officers. Branded retailers, like

Table 2.1 The Public, Private, and Secret Self model divides dress into nine categories.

	Reality dress	Fun/leisure dress	Fantasy dress
Public self	Gender Uniforms Business wear	Office parties Dating Sports events Reenactors' public performances	Halloween Living history Festivals Reenactors' public performances
Private self	Housework Gardening Novelty items	Home Exercise	Childhood memories Sensual lingerie
Secret self	Tight underwear	Some tattoos Novelty underwear	Sexual fantasies Assume another persona

Source: Eicher J. B., & Miller, K. A. (1994), Dress and the public, private and secret self: Revisiting a model. *ITAA Proceedings*, Proceedings of the International Textile and Apparel Association, Inc., p. 145.

Abercrombie and Fitch or Top Shop, may require their employees to dress in the clothing they sell. Some governments have general rules of public dressing, such as outlawing nudity in public places, but other governments may be more specific. In Saudi Arabia, all female citizens must cover their bodies. This rule is both governmental and religious. In the Islamic faith, women wear an abaya, or outer coat, when in public. Islamic faith dictates that women dress modestly in public and cover themselves so that men unrelated to them may not gaze upon them. The abaya is usually worn with a veil. The niqāb is a veil common in Arabian countries; it is a black square of cloth that covers the head and face, with a slit for the eyes. The burqa or chadri is a form of abaya common in central Asian countries; it covers the body and contains a grill or net for the eyes. This conforms to the idea of dressing at the public level. However, in private, the wearer may remove the public dress to reveal the private level of dress. This level of dress is only seen by female friends or female and male relatives, and may be fashionable, but is always modest.

Dressing for the secret self can be hidden and not seen by anyone else; generally, undergarments fall into this category. A man who likes wearing women's underwear because he likes the silky feel but does not let anyone know of his preference is dressing at the secret self level. But the secret self can also be revealed to others, typically in the form of fantasy or escapist dress. A person may wear a superhero costume publically, but keep secret the desire to *be* the superhero (Miller-Spillman, 2013).

Anthropologist and Star Wars fan Eirik Saethre has fond memories of playing with *Star Wars* action figures when he was a child. He enjoyed the films and liked the imaginative play associated with the toys. As an adult he found a group of other adults, the 501st Legion, who recreate and dress as Stormtroopers. Although the 501st Legion demonstrates in public, Saethre, and likely others, harbor the secret desire to *be* the action figure. He proceeded to build a suit and soon learned there were specific guidelines to follow. By following the guidelines, Saethre not only was constructing a costume, he was also constructing a new identity. He wrote, "In constructing a kit, prospective members [of the 501st Legion] were also constructing a boundary between themselves and the 'average person' or 'casual fan' " (2013, p. 498). He argued that in the process of acquiring a specific language and specific aesthetic code, he developed a new identity for himself. This new identity coincided with the secret self x fantasy cell of the Public, Private, and Secret Self model: assuming another persona.

Body image

Body image is defined as "a person's perceptions, thoughts, and feelings about his or her body" (Grogan, 2008, 3). How a person perceives his or her body affects how he or she feels about it and consequently how he or she dresses it. Mostly, people dress to hide perceived flaws and use aesthetics (see this chapter) to draw attention away from the perceived flaw and to something else. A person may camouflage acne scars with make-up, wear slimming undergarments to achieve a smoother silhouette, or wear a boldly-colored scarf to draw attention to his or her face. Body image is linked to self-esteem, such that the better/worse a person feels about his or her body the better/worse his or her self-esteem (Grogan, 2008; Pope, Phillips & Olivardia, 2000). Feeling poor about one's body can result in body dissatisfaction. When people are dissatisfied with their bodies they take measures to change them.

The processes people take in order to create an appearance are called **appearance management behaviors**. Appearance management behaviors are classified into two categories: routine and non-routine (Rudd & Lennon, 2000). Routine appearance management behaviors are frequent procedures that carry little to no health risk, such as ironing clothing, wearing make-up, and exercise. Non-routine appearance management behaviors are engaged in less frequently and carry some degree of risk or pain, such as tattooing, liposuction, anorexia, bulimia, or chronic dieting. Reilly and Rudd (2009) found non-routine appearance management behaviors to be related to social anxiety among women, such that as women experience more social anxiety they are more likely to use a risky or painful procedure. Reilly and Rudd believe that non-routine appearance management behaviors are perceived to provide a quick fix to the perceived problem.

Sometimes, a person's perceptions of their body may not reflect reality which can lead to appearance-related disorders such as anorexia nervosa, bulimia nervosa, or chronic dieting. Anorexia nervosa is the refusal to eat food while bulimia nervosa is bingeing on food and then vomiting it; both result in unhealthy weight loss. It is estimated that 1% of the female population in general suffer with an eating disorder (Anorexia Bulimia Care, n.d.), while other research estimates that 20 million women in the United States suffer with an eating disorder at some point in their life (Wade, Keski-Rahkonen, & Hudson, 2011). While there are numerous reasons that a person may suffer from an eating disorder (e.g., abuse, trauma, teasing, bullying) many people also blame the fashion industry because it perpetrates an unrealistic thin standard for women. Model Coco Rocha recalls being told by modeling agents, "The look this year is anorexic. We don't want you to be anorexic, just look it" (Misener, 2011). She was 15 at the time. Researchers found that between 2001 and 2002 the average dimension of British women's waist had increased by 7 inches since 1951; in 1951 the average waist size was 27 inches, but in 2013 it was 34 inches, while bust size remained relatively the same (Winter & McDermott, 2013). However, models have become thinner since the 1960s. In the 1950s idealized female forms were voluptuous and hourglass, but in the 1960s slim models like Twiggy began to appear and models became thinner and thinner (Grogan, 2008). Grogan writes, in the mid-1990s, "designers and magazine editors often chose to use extremely thin models such as Kate Moss to advertise their clothes and beauty products. The late 1990s saw the rise of 'heroin chic'; that is fashion houses made very thin models up to look like stereotypical heroin users" (p. 23). Former Australian *Vogue* editor Kirstie Clements (2013) recounts models skipping meals, using an intravenous (IV) drip, and eating tissues to stave off hunger pains. Striving to be thin (and hired) has resulted in models dying from lack of nutrition. In 1996 American model Margaux Hemingway died, in 2006 Brazilian model Ana Carolina Reston died, in 2006 Uruguayan model Lusiel Ramos died, in 2007 her sister Eliana Ramos died, in 2010 French model Isabel Caro died. Their deaths have been attributed to eating disorders.

Part of the drive for thinness can be attributed to the fashion industry using younger and younger models. Established, "mature" models in their early 20s are competing with models in their teens, whose bodies have yet to fully develop. In an effort to compete the older models try extreme measures to stay thin. At the age of 13 Elle Fanning became a model for Marc Jacobs and at the age of 14 Hailee Steinfeld became a model for Miu Miu. In 2011 French *Vogue* used model Thylane Blondeau in one of its issues. She wore sexy clothing. Her hair was done up and her face applied with make-up. Her poses were provocative. She was 10 years old.

Public outcry has resulted in some changes in the modeling industry. Madrid Fashion Week instituted a minimum body mass index (BMI, a ratio of height to weight that indicates healthiness), as have Milan Fashion Week and Israel Fashion Week. In 2012 the international *Vogue* magazines vowed to ban models under the age of 16 and any model with signs of an eating disorder.

Men also are prone to body image issues and can suffer from body dissatisfaction. Prior to the 1990s, men were generally portrayed in the media as having average bodies, with a few exceptions. Underwear was advertised sans body, in packages and not on models. One of the first underwear ads to feature a muscular model was Calvin Klein's racy underwear campaign featuring a very muscular and toned Mark Wahlberg. More fashion campaigns using muscular, almost-nude men followed. In addition, performance-enhancements, such as anabolic steroids, have contributed to unprecedented muscle growth and size. But men needed not to just be muscular, they also needed to be lean. Thus, men became dissatisfied with their bodies two ways—the desire to lose weight and the desire to gain weight (Pope, Phillips, & Olivardia, 2000).

It is estimated that 10–15% of people who suffer from eating disorders are men (National Association of Anorexia Nervosa and Associated Disorders, n.d.). The percentage may actually be higher because men are socialized to not worry about their appearance and if they do to not talk about it. In addition to anorexia nervosa, bulimia nervosa, and chronic dieting, men with body dissatisfaction also can suffer from muscle dysmorphia, sometimes called "reverse anorexia." Men with muscle dysmorphia see their bodies as under-developed, where in actuality their bodies are very muscular. They often engage in regimens of obsessive weight-training in order to increase muscle size.

Just as with women, there are many reasons why men experience appearance-related disorders, including the fashion industry and affiliated media. In the early 2000s Hedi Slimane began designing "skinny" silhouettes for Dior Homme, which became highly fashionable and replicated by many other designers in the industry. The skinny look shifted the fashionable male body aesthetic from big and buff to slim. Today, as men strive to fit into skinny clothes and are impacted by fashion advertisements of skinny models, they no doubt internalize the look and seek ways to alter their body shape.

Aesthetic perception and learning is based on the assumption that people need to learn to appreciate and understand beauty. Aesthetics is the rules of beauty. Every culture, society, or individual has their own beliefs as to what makes something beautiful or ugly or somewhere in between. Designers work with the elements of aesthetics to create their looks: color, line, form, space, and texture. These elements can be used in different ways, known as principles: repetition, sequence, alternation, gradation, transition, contrast, proportion and balance. Thus, colors can be alternated in a striped shirt, textures can contrast in a skirt, or lines can transition from horizontal or vertical in a blazer. The theory posits people have to learn to understand the interplay of elements and principles in order to appreciate beauty. A person may not like vertical stripes personally, but understanding that according to westernized rules of aesthetics, a vertical line elongates the body and a long, lean body is valued over a wide body can change the person's perception of vertical stripes. A person may not like the color green but understanding that a green coat on a person with red hair brightens the hair color may be appreciated.

Researchers and scholars have devised different models to explain how aesthetics are perceived. Dress scholar Marilyn Delong (1998) approaches aesthetics as formal, expressive, and symbolic qualities. *Formal qualities* are the elements and principles of design, *expressive qualities* are the emotions associated with wearing the apparel product, and *symbolic qualities* are meanings associated with the apparel product. The combination of these three influences the wearer's appreciation of the garment.

Using a pearl necklace as an example, we can analyze the formal, expressive, and symbolic qualities to better appreciate its aesthetics. The formal qualities of the pearl necklace are repeated round shape, lustrous white color, and smooth texture. The expressive qualities might be making the wearer feel sophisticated. The symbolic qualities might be reference to the month in which the wearer was born (the birthstone for the month of June is pearl). Thus, the pearl necklace is perceived as a combination of three qualities.

Another scholar of the social-psychology of dress, Mary Lynn Damhorst (1989, 2005), developed a model that envisions aesthetic perception as a series of embedded elements or networks (see Figure 2.2). At the center of the model are the perceptual elements such as line, shape, form, color, etc. This is encompassed by the condition of the material. The condition of the material is encompassed by the treatment of the materials, and so on. Using this model we understand that the aesthetic elements are situated within concentric series of cultural, social, and personal spheres.

When a new collection is offered by a designer the consumer (or viewer) has to understand how the aesthetics relate to each other. A viewer learns to appreciate a design that is different (but not too different) from previous designs. Repeated exposure to the design helps the appreciation and acceptance process (see mere exposure hypothesis in Chapter 5).

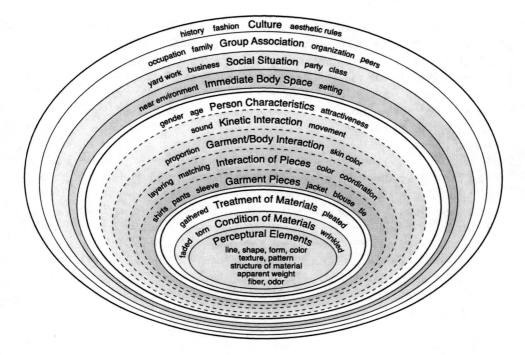

Figure 2.2 Damhorst's model of the many influences of clothing meaning is used to understand the many influences on clothing. Image courtesy of Mary Lynn Damhorst and Fairchild Books.

In the 1950s, during which Dior's New Look was sweeping across Europe and North America, British designers were advocating for simpler styles and wanted to establish "good" standards of taste (see Chapter 3 for more on the concept of taste). The Council for Industrial Design was one group established to educate consumers and fashion industry professionals about appropriate designs. "The programme of regulation was managed by institutions ... and involved in campaigning to change the attitudes of both manufactures and the consumer, and the production of propaganda 'aimed at familiarizing the public with that new concept "design" ' " (Partington, 1992, p. 153, quoting Sparke, 1986, p. 65). The aim of the program, as Partington notes, was to educate working-class women on tasteful aesthetics and promote useful, utilitarian designs over the elaborate, decorative New Look fashion. Sensible styles were displayed in public exhibitions and publications explained how to combine aesthetics appropriately. Some developments of the utilitarian style became popular, like the shirtwaister and multipurpose suit. "As the consumer of fashion goods, the working-class women were being educated in the skills of 'good taste' (restraint, practicality, etc.)" (Partington, 1992, p. 155).

Likewise, in the 1990s fashion designers began offering collections that were simpler from the previous decade. The 1980s were awash with frenzied patterns of bold strokes and vivid colors. Designers like Nolan Miller and Christian Lacroix used an abundance of sequins and rhinestones and yards of shiny fabrics to dress their clients. The look was obvious, in-your-face luxe; it screamed glamour; it was far from subtle. But in the 1990s designers like Donna Karan, Calvin Klein, and Giorgio Armani were offering collections that were much simpler, with the flash and decoration removed. These designers had always offered simper clothing, but perceptions of aesthetics and its symbolic qualities shifted and people began wearing plain clothes. Some people supposed this trend to be boring. Rather, they needed to examine the aesthetics and relative meaning to appreciate the look. "Designers wanted to move away from the ostentation and the perceived bad taste of the gilt logo which was seen as too blatant a symbol of wealth and excess" (Arnold, 2000, p. 169). The simplified cuts from Donna Karan, Calvin Klein, Giorgio Armani and others, made from fabrics of neutral colors like black, navy, and white, were a new aesthetic that needed to be learned to be appreciated. Through magazine and newspaper editorials, advertisements, and retail promotions, people soon realized/learned that simplicity equaled luxury and luxury equaled an emphasis on fabric, cut, and silhouette, not on decoration and adornment.

Shifting Erogenous Zones

Historian James Laver (1969) first proposed a **Theory of Shifting Erogenous Zones** to explain why fashions go in and out of style. He was influenced by psychologist J. C. Flugel (1930) who argued that the naked body is anti-erotic. The naked body is anti-erotic because it leaves nothing to the imagination. The imagination is more powerful than reality. For example, in horror films, storylines where the monster is not depicted or only slightly depicted on screen tend to be more frightening because your imagination can conjure the type of monster that scares you. Simultaneously, the anticipation of seeing the monster builds. Frequently, when the monster is finally seen there is a bit of a disappointment because it does not match your expectations. Likewise, a clothed body allows for imagination and anticipation. Based on this premise, Laver argued that styles of women's fashion change in order to reveal different body parts. As the body part is exposed, it becomes eroticized. Showing what was previously hidden becomes exciting until it becomes a common sight. When a particular body part becomes overexposed it is no longer sexually enticing, so a new area of the body is exposed.

In the early 1900s women's breasts were thrust up with corsets and brassieres and their legs were covered, but in the 1920s women's legs were eroticized when they threw off their floor-length dresses for loose dresses that rose to the knee, yet the breast was covered and flattened. In the 1930s hemlines dropped but the back of women was frequently exposed. Thus, what became eroticized shifted over time. (See Figures 2.3, 2.4, and 2.5.)

Figure 2.3 The Ohio State University Historic Costume and Textiles Collection, courtesy of Dr. Anne Bissonnette.

Figure 2.4 University of Hawai'i Historic Costume Museum.

Figure 2.5 The Theory of Shifting Erogenous Zones posits that fashions change in order to expose different body parts. In the 1930s the back was fashionable to expose (2.3), while this asymmetrical dress from the 1970s shows how an exposed shoulder was fashionable (2.4); by the 2010s the leg became the new focal point (2.5). Nata Sha/Shutterstock.com.

Yet, fashion historian Valerie Steele (1985) noted that the theory can also apply to covered areas of the body that are enhanced or exaggerated through clothing, not just what is revealed. Poulaines, also called Crakows (they were popular in Crakow, Poland), were very long, pointed men's shoes fashionable in 15th century Europe. One could either read the shoe as an erotic fascination with feet or symbolic substitution for the size of the wearer's phallus. In the 16th century, the phallus itself was also emphasized by using a codpiece, a piece of fabric that covered the groin where men's hose were joined together. Likewise, women's body parts were emphasized similarly. The bustle of the 19th century brought attention to the derrière, while shoulder pads highlighted shoulders in the 1940s and 1980s, and the waist was (de)emphasized via corsets in the 1950s. Like the examples of the exposed body, apparel fashions have changed to force attention on areas that are considered erotic or fetishistic.

Laver's argument was based on the social structure of gender and the economic dependence of women on men. His argument was that women must keep men interested in order to financially support them and they accomplish this by exposing different parts of their body. Some people argue that the theory is dead because women have more economic independence than before, that with today's styles the entire body has been over exposed, and that there are reasons other than sexuality to adopt and discard styles of dress. While these arguments may be true, one cannot argue that the desire to attract a mate is gone. The theory is still valid in its basic premise that fashions change to alleviate boredom and overexposure, whether or not the motivation is to attract a spouse. In the 1980s midcrop shirts that revealed toned abdomens were popular. In the early 2010s asymmetrical tops for women revealed sexy shoulders. In fact, in the early 2010s Old Navy advertised the "high-water" pants with a campaign that asked people to "show off their sexy ankles." Perhaps we have come full-circle from the antebellum days when the ankle was erotic in the pre-Civil War Southern United States?

With change in the economic status of women—and men now needing to offer women more than a monetary enticement—men's fashion has seen changes in exposing erogenous zones. Shirts changed from t-shirts to tank tops to expose arms, and necklines shifted from crew to v-neck to deep-v to display male cleavage (or "he-vage"). Shorts, as they rose and fell from hot-pants to mid-thigh to knee-length to Capri-length served to draw focus to the groin, thigh, knee, and calf, respectively. Likewise, sock length also called attention to particular body parts; the sockless or no-see-sock look reveals ankles, while different lengths focus attention on the calf or knee.

With today's fashions focusing on heightened body exposure, the body can still be eroticized through tattoos and piercings. Both are erotic features of adornment because they draw attention to the flesh and by consequence to a portion of the body. The location of tattoos on the body have shifted over time and in recent decades it has been fashionable for men to have tattoos around one's bicep, lower back, and upper arm (i.e., irezumi) (Reilly, in press). Popularity in piercing sites, too, changed from ear lobes to ear cartilage, to ear tragus, to nipples, navels and back of neck. It can be argued that the locations of the tattoos or piercings change because of overexposure and the need for something unique.

One can see a relationship between this theory and Historic Continuity theory (this chapter) in that both theories argue that people become bored with the status quo and seek change. The theory of historic continuity argues that this change needs to be small, resulting in an evolution of fashion, while the theory of shifting erogenous zones argues a new body part needs to be exposed.

Historic Continuity theory

Fashion is a careful balance between wearing what is similar to others but also what is different. People desire change (in order to be unique or to alleviate boredom) but they are more comfortable with small changes than large changes. A large change is too abrupt and too different. If you were in a hot sauna and then suddenly jumped into an icy pond, you would be in shock. It is similar with fashion; going from one extreme to another is too jolting, but a gradual change is tolerable. Styles will change in small ways in order to satisfy the need for difference but not alienate the psyche that needs familiarity.

Historic Continuity theory explains that a detail about fashion will change over seasons until it has reached its maximum (or minimum) and then reverse order until it reaches its minimum (or maximum). It will continue on this pendulum and create fashion cycles. A skirt's hemline will continue to rise until it cannot be raised anymore (it has reached its endpoint), then reverse order and continue to lower until it cannot fall anymore (reached another endpoint), and reverse again. Anthropologist Alfred L. Kroeber (1919) was one of the first researchers to examine the phenomenon of fashion change using Historic Continuity theory and concluded that styles change slowly from one extreme to another. He likened this to a pendulum on a clock swinging back and forth. He found that a skirt length will recur approximately at 35 year intervals and that skirt width returned after an interval of 100 years.

Other researchers have continued this line of research and examined skirt length (Curran, 1999), décolleté, waist and skirt length/width (Lowe & Lowe, 1982, 1985; Richardson & Kroeber, 1940), men's hair styles (Pedersen, 2001; Robinson, 1976), and details of men's pants, shirts, and jackets (Reilly, 2007). (See Figure 2.6.) In general, they have found fashion change tends to follow a path; men's shirt collars widen and slim down; hemlines rise and fall; waists rise and fall. Researchers John W. G. Lowe and Elizabeth D. Lowe (1985) found that although dimensions (e.g., silhouettes) are cyclical, style is not. In addition, they argued, dimensions may not return to the maximum before reversing. Andrew Reilly (2007) similarly argued that with regard to menswear, fashion dimensions are evolutionary though not

45

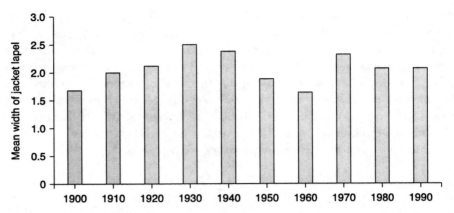

Figure 2.6 This graph illustrates how the width of men's jacket lapels has evolved over the 20th century. Reilly, A. (2008), Fashion cycles in men's jackets, dress shirts, and slacks. In A. Reilly & S. Cosbey (Eds), *Men's Fashion Reader* (pp. 525–537). New York: Fairchild.

cyclical, meaning that they evolve from the prior fashion but do not recur at regular intervals.

This phenomenon can be observed in other fashion details as well. Observe the fit of pants. In the late 1970s "French jeans" were extraordinarily tight but through the 1980s the fit of jeans had become more relaxed until the 1990s when they were loose and baggy. Then the trend reversed and they became skin-tight again by the 2010s. Adults were even shopping in children and young adult departments in order to get the tightest pair of jeans they could find. The arrival of jeggings (leggings that were printed with a denim look) helped facilitate the desire for a tight silhouette. Then in 2011 Dior and Lanvin offered an extremely radical silhouette. One Dior pair of men's pants had a leg opening of 24 inches. Granted, the shift was too radical to be adopted en masse, but those desirous of change began to wear pants that had a looser fit than before. By 2013 Ferragamo also offered wide legged pants for men. Corollary to this is the waist location of pants. In the 1980s, a high waist was fashionable but it dropped by the 1990s. Low pants were in and showing off one's underwear or derrière was a common feature. By 2012, the waistline of pants had fallen so low that it could not fall any lower and still maintain coverage so the waistline began to rise, with Prada offering early versions of this trend.

There is an exception to the rule that change must be gradual. Twice in history there has been a radical change that did not follow the projected trend. After the French Revolution (1787–1799), women's fashions changed from ornate, large, cumbersome styles to flowing, softer styles. After World War II (1939–1945), women's fashion changed from restricted, masculine and tubular silhouettes to wide, voluminous, and feminine styles. Both of these abrupt changes in fashion were due to significant changes in social and political structure. France had changed from a monarchy to a democracy after 12 years of brutal battles, and after World War II the western world was emerging from five years of restrictions on fabric and an upset in gender relationships. Thus, the exception is that during times of great change or social upheaval there may be a sudden upheaval in the direction of a fashion trend.

Symbolic Interaction theory

Symbolic Interaction theory acts as a bridge between the individual and society. It explains how the individual makes sense of meanings and symbols via social interaction. Philosopher George Herbert Mead (1967) is credited with the development of this theory though students of Mead such as Herbert Blumer (1969) have greatly contributed to the theory and established three principles of symbolic interaction: 1. People give meaning to things and behave towards the thing based on the meaning they give. 2. Meanings are based on social interaction. 3. Meanings are interpreted by the person. This theory means that people use symbols to interact with each other and those symbols are created by, and interpreted by, the person. The theory posits that people are not interacting with the object per se, but with what they believe the object means. Thus, when you meet a stranger in a police uniform, you are reacting to what the police uniform means to you, not necessarily the uniform itself. To some people the uniform could mean safety; to others it could mean oppression.

If we tie this idea to fashion we can surmise that people ascribe meanings to articles of dress. Recall in the discussion of semiotics (Chapter 1, p. 19) that communication is derived from a signifier and a signified, which is governed by a code. With this in mind, consider this example. You are vacationing in Honolulu and become lost. You need directions for how to get back to your hotel and you come across two people: a woman in a police uniform and a woman in a floral Hawaiian shirt, khaki shorts, and sandals worn with black socks. You interpret the woman in the uniform as a member of the police force, based on prior experience. Similarly, based on experience you interpret the other woman as a tourist. Your past experience informs you that police are knowledgeable, but that tourists are not because they do not live in the area. You ask the police officer where to find your hotel and she gives you accurate directions. This social interaction reinforces your belief that people in police uniforms are knowledgeable, and aligns with Davis' (1982) assertion that meanings need to be maintained or revised. If you had asked to the woman you perceive to be a tourist and she gave you accurate directions, your assumptions about the meaning of Hawaiian shirts worn with sandals and socks would be challenged and you would likely revise your interpretation; tourists might be knowledgeable.

Interpreting the meaning of dress also depends on the context. In the above example, the context was a vacation spot. This likely influenced the perception of police officers and tourists. However, if the context was different—a different historical time, a different culture—like Nazi Germany, your interpretation of police officers might be different—fear rather than trust.

Likewise, context also helps to decipher **ambiguous** messages. The word "read" is ambiguous by itself; is it a future tense verb or past tense verb? You need the context of other words to decipher its meaning: "Last night I *read* a book" or "Tonight I will *read* a book." Likewise, situational context helps you decipher the meaning of particular dress. In European and American societies, wedding dresses are traditionally white; the color white is associated with purity. If you saw a bride in a red wedding dress, you might be confused because red is associated with wantonness (among other interpretations). You might think, what is the meaning of a red wedding dress; why is it not white? The context of the situation will help resolve the ambiguity. You notice that the ceremony is spoken in Mandarin Chinese and the bride appears to be of Chinese ethnicity, and then you remember red is the traditional color for wedding dresses in many Asian countries because the color red is associated with happiness. The context provided you the cues you needed to interpret the clothing.

Dress scholars Susan Kaiser, Richard Nagasawa, and Sandra Hutton (1997) surmise that ambivalence and ambiguity are important components that contribute to changing trends. **Ambivalence** is the feeling of being conflicted or drawn in multiple directions. You might feel *ambivalence* on a Friday night when you want to go to see a movie but also want to study for an exam. An *ambiguity*, as discussed, is the state of having multiple interpretations or meanings; the intended meaning is not clear or is confusing. The combination of both ambivalence and ambiguity allows for multiple interpretations and a "dialogue" with society to determine which interpretation will prevail. If an interpretation prevails, the authors argue, then the style will become a fashion; if an interpretation does not prevail and a style remains ambiguous in its meaning, then the style will be discarded.

Through the 20th century, the black leather jacket held both ambivalent and ambiguous meanings in American and European societies due to shifting changes in male identity. Meanings generated by wearing the black leather jacket were due to:

> [A] degree of creative tension in the interaction of the relationships of form, viewer, and context. The black leather jacket owes much of its status as a symbol to this image manipulation in connection with certain creative tensions associated with male identity: gay or straight, rugged protector or individualist survivor, hero or antihero, powerful or vulnerable, and tribal or mainstream fashion. (DeLong & Park, 2008: 171)

Kaiser, Nagasawa, and Hutton (1997) argue that all people experience ambivalence and that products produced in capitalist marketplaces (such as America and Europe) express ambivalence. The black leather jacket thus expressed the ambivalence of male identity. As the black leather jacket was worn by different male archetypical groups it created ambiguous meanings that needed to be negotiated within society. Successful negotiations of meaning rely on general consensus.

Dress scholars Marilyn DeLong and Juyeon Park (2008) noted that the black leather jacket was a symbol of military chic style in Germany during World War I, changed to total military power in World War II Germany, but perceived as brave when adopted by American military officers during World War II. The context of who was wearing, who was interpreting, and the historic timeframe contributed to interpreting the black leather jacket as different symbols. DeLong and Park further surmised that during the 1960s the black leather jacket became a symbol of teenage rebellion due to films where antiheroes adorned it, but in the 1970s became a symbol of a "cool" yet functioning member of society when the character of Fonzie wore it in the American television series *Happy Days* (1974–1984). Lastly, DeLong and Park argue that the black leather jacket shifted from "tribal" or subcultural fashion to mainstream fashion by the end of the 20th century when people from all levels of society adopted it.

Thus, the black leather jacket represents an example of symbolic interaction. Ambivalence of male identity created ambiguous meanings that needed to be clarified. Meanings were assigned to the jacket; meanings were based on social interaction; and interpreted given the situational context.

BOXED CASE 2.1: ONE INDIVIDUAL STARTS A TREND

Jayanada Nandini Devi was the wife of a civil servant in Bombay (today called Mumbai) and a prominent citizen in her own right. She is identified as the source of the "Nivi" style of sari draping originating in 1866 (Tu, 2009). Traditional saris are lengths of cloth that are unstitched and uncut, as dictated by Hindi custom. During Devi's life, saris were draped around the body in different styles according to region, often with uncovered breasts. Given her status as a prominent person, Devi wanted something modest (to align with new ideas coming from colonialism) and something that was non-regional. She adopted a choli (a stitched bodice) and a skirt, with the sari draped over her left arm and shoulder (see Figure 2.7). The style was adopted by other women and was disseminated on a broader, national scale in the 1930s though the Hindi film industry (Dwyer & Patel, 2002). The style was free of regional identity and modest (e.g., the breasts were covered) and took on the meaning of a unified nation as well as a modern woman during the Indian national movement for independence (Tu, 2009). Today the Nivi style is prominent, has been worn by other leaders such as Mahatma Gandhi, and is perceived by outsiders to be the traditional form of Indian dress.

Figure 2.7 The Nivi style of draping the sari around the body was created 1866 by Jayanda Nandini Devi. paffy/Shutterstock.com.

BOXED CASE 2.2: FASHION LEADERS: CELEBRITIES AND FASHION

Celebrities wield enormous power due to their elevated status, and are often viewed as authorities on different subjects. Celebrities have the ability to start a trend simply by wearing a garment, acting as a paid spokesperson, or, more recently, launching their own fashion brand. Jaclyn Smith (actress in *Charlie's Angels*, 1976–1981) was one of the earliest celebrities to launch a fashion line with her collection of clothing for K-Mart in 1985. Other celebrities such as Russell Simmons, Jessica Simpson, and Beyonce have also found success in the fashion industry. Now, many are branching out into fragrances.

Celebrity fragrances had a brief life in the 1980s, most notably with Uninhibited from Cher, but today's plethora of celebrity fragrances can be traced back to Jennifer Lopez's Glow by J. Lo in 2002. In its first year it sold $200 million globally (Gordon, 2012) and since then the singer has launched over a dozen more fragrances. Her success is likely what influenced other celebrities to enter the fragrance market, such as Hilary Duff, Justin Beiber, Taylor Swift, Antonio Banderas, Lady Gaga, Jennifer Aniston, Halle Berry, Paris Hilton, Bruce Willis, Gwen Stefani, David Beckham, Tim McGraw, Britney Spears, Katy Perry, Jessica Simpson, Selena Gomez, Nicki Minaj, and Rhianna (see Figure 2.8).

Figure 2.8 Reb'l Fleur by singer Rihanna is just one of the many celebrity fragrances on the market. s_buckley/Shutterstock.com.

According to fragrance marketer Miranda Gordon (2012) celebrities are entering the fragrance market because it is lucrative. Compared to apparel lines, where you need different sizes, different fits, and different markets, fragrances have the one-size-fits-all ability to cross different markets. However, she says only a few are involved in the actual development of the fragrance.

Summary

The individual's influence on fashion stems from choices one makes, one's desire to be unique, and one's role as a fashion leader. The desire to be different—to stand out from the crowd—motivates some people to wear aesthetic combinations that are unusual or peculiar. If the person is someone whom other people seek out for advice on fashion and clothing, that person's choices can influence others' style of dress. However, as people change their modes of dress, they prefer small changes rather than abrupt, big changes. This accounts for a linear or evolutional explanation for fashion change. Dressing at the individual level is about satisfying a personal need or desire. The desire may be to excite others, demonstrate a different understanding of aesthetics, or live out a secret fantasy. At the most personal, a person can change their body to achieve a unique appearance. But it is important to remember that dress is imbued with meaning that is negotiated with society.

Key Terms

- Adoption and diffusion model
- Aesthetic perception and learning
- Ambiguous
- Ambivalence
- Appearance management behaviors
- Body image
- Expressive qualities
- Fashion communicators

- Fashion innovators
- Formal qualities
- Historic continuity
- Public, Private, and Secret Self model
- Shifting erogenous zones
- Symbolic interaction
- Symbolic qualities
- Uniqueness

Discussion questions

1. Using the Public, Private, and Secret Self model, identify examples of each cell that pertain to your dressing behaviors.
2. Identify a new fashion leader. This can be someone in class, school, community, or a celebrity. Discuss why this person is a fashion leader, what style the person endorses, and

how you think s/he will influence fashion in the next three seasons. Now, identify a fashion leader whose influence has waned. What was this person noted for and why do you think his/her influence has fallen?

3. What celebrities have tried to influence fashion but did not succeed? Why do you think they failed where others have triumphed?
4. Do you think the theory of shifting erogenous zones is still relevant?
5. What ways have you alleviated boredom when you dressed?

Learning activities

1. Wear something unique and outlandish for a day. Visit different venues, such as school, a retail outlet, and a grocery store. How do people react to you? How do you feel wearing something that garners attention?
2. Bring in a celebrity fragrance to class. Discuss the scent and the flaçon (bottle) and packaging. How does it relate to that celebrity's image?
3. You will need magazines or images from a specific past decade for this activity. Collect data on the length of shorts to chart a trend. You can collect data in one of two ways: (1) if the model is standing and you can see from the waist to foot, measure the distance from waist to foot, measure the distance from waist to hem of the shorts, and calculate a ratio; or (2) divide the leg into different areas, for example upper thigh, mid-thigh, just above the knee, and mid-calf. You and a friend will look at each image and determine to which category the image belongs. Keep a record of your data by year. Illustrate your results using a simple bar graph for each year. Based on your findings, predict how that trend will continue or recede. An alternative to this could be measuring the height of socks, using the following categories: below ankle, above ankle, mid-calf, and above calf/ under knee.
4. Use Damhorst's model depicted in Figure 2.2 to analyze a garment from your wardrobe.

Further reading

Gibson, P. C. (2012). *Fashion and the Celebrity Culture*. Oxford: Berg.

Katz, E., & Lazarsfeld, P. F. (2009). *Personal Influence: The Part Played by People in the Flow of Mass Communications*. New Brunswick, New Jersey: Transaction Publishers.

Knight, D., & Kim, E. Y. (2007). Japanese consumers' need for uniqueness: Effects on brand perceptions and purchase intention. *Journal of Fashion Marketing and Management, 11* (2), 270–280.

Laver, J. (1969). *Modesty in Dress: An Inquiry into the Fundamentals of Fashion*. Boston: Houghton Mifflin Company.

Mazzeo, T. J. (2010). *The Secret of Chanel No. 5: The Intimate History of the World's Most Famous Perfume*. New York City: HarperCollins.

Studak, C. M., & Workman, J. E. (2004). Fashion groups, gender, and boredom proneness. *International Journal of Consumer Studies, 28* (1), 66–74.

Tu, R. (2009). Dressing the nation: Indian cinema costume and the making of a national fashion, 1947–1957. In E. Paulicelli, and H. Clark, *The Fabric of Cultures: Fashion, Identity, and Globalization* (pp. 28–40). New York City: Routledge.

FASHION AND SOCIETY

Society is based on the grouping of people together by some common trait, such as skin color, amount of money possessed, genealogy, or type of work performed. The role of society is for people with similar qualities or interests to support each other. In the European Middle Ages, feudalism was a type of society where people were categorized as land owners, merchants, and peasants. Similarly, in India the caste system divided people into four classes and in South Africa, under apartheid law, the population was separated based on racial laws. University society is divided into faculty, staff, administration, undergraduate and graduate strata and within each are further divisions (e.g., tenured, tenure-track, freshmen, sophomore, junior, senior, masters, doctoral). Each of these social strata developed their own rules of behavior and expectations. It is probably easy for you to recognize freshmen from doctoral students or people in different majors based on their habits and style of dressing. The unspoken but learned rules for people within the society are called habitus.

Habitus is a term coined by philosopher Pierre Bourdieu (1990) to explain learned behaviors that are taken for granted, but nonetheless indicate "appropriateness." You may have never thought about why you eat with a fork, spoon, and knife. If someone were to eat with their hands or fingers you would probably think them uncivilized, but in the Middle East it is proper to eat with one's hands. If you were to visit and began to eat with your left hand you would be considered barbaric because it is only acceptable to eat with your right hand (the left hand is considered unhygienic). Another example is removing shoes when entering a home. In many westernized homes guests retain their shoes when entering a house, because to remove one's shoes without permission is considered rude. Yet, the opposite is true in many Eastern homes, where it is expected that guests remove shoes before entering the house, because shoes are considered dirty. Bourdieu argued that common acts like these become part of the structure of society and are deeply ingrained in the subconscious. A result of habitus is the development of aesthetic taste (Bourdieu, 1984).

Taste is a matter of aesthetic liking and appreciating. If you were invited to a reception at the White House or Buckingham Palace or the court of Japan, you would likely dress in a ball gown or tuxedo or formal kimono because you have learned that for formal occasions these dress forms are desired and necessary. While at the reception if you saw a guest dressed in jeans and a t-shirt, you might think, "that is bad taste." Bourdieu (1984) believed that judgments of taste are in themselves judgments about social position. A judgment about good taste versus bad taste is in fact a judgment about social class—that is, the values and ways of one class are preferred over the values and ways of another class. He argued that children are taught appropriate taste for their class and to reject taste of other classes. The children then carry their leanings about taste into adulthood. Thus, when judging the informally-attired guest at the reception, you not only think the jeans and t-shirt are inappropriate but also indicative of an inferior social standing. Likewise, Figure 3.1 demonstrates a violation of good taste by wearing socks with sandals. For many people in America, wearing socks with sandals is considered tacky or classless. The man in the image perhaps never learned this rule or is from a society where wearing socks with sandals is socially appropriate.

Historian James Laver (1973) hypothesized that taste in fashion is related to its "in-ness." He offered a guideline to demonstrate how fashions are perceived relative to the Zeitgeist (see Chapter 4, p. 80, for further explanation). When a style is 10 years too soon or "before its time" it is considered indecent; at five years too soon it is shameless; at one year too soon it is daring; the fashion "today" is "in fashion" or "smart." That fashion one year later is dowdy; 10 years later is hideous; 20 years later is ridiculous; 30 years later is amusing; 50 years later is quaint; 70 years later is

Figure 3.1 This man exhibits what some call bad taste by violating learned and expected social rules that prohibit wearing socks with sandals. Lobke Peers/Shutterstock.com.

charming; 100 years later is romantic; and 150 years later is beautiful. These designations may also explain why some styles are revived from history (see "Historic resurrection" theory, Chapter 5, p. 107), because as time passes they are viewed with a different eye and could serve to be relevant again.

Also central to this chapter is the consumer demand model. This economic model posits that when prices are high there is little demand for the object being offered; however, as prices begin to decrease the demand increases. We can see this model in action when a new fashion collection is offered. Typically, new styles are higher in price than existing styles that have been available in the market for a while. As time passes, the price will fall (retailers want to sell them to make room for new stock) and more people will buy the style. This pattern continues until the price reaches its lowest-offered point and the style is sold out.

However, as economist Harvey Leibenstein (1950) articulated, there are some variations of this theory. He identified a Veblen effect, snob effect, and bandwagon effect, which contradict the classic consumer demand model. A **Veblen effect** is when more people purchase a product as the price increases. The **snob effect** is when preference for a product increases when the supply becomes limited. And the **bandwagon effect** is when preference for a product increases as more people adopt the product. These effects are influenced by personality traits of the consumer. Status consumption influences the Veblen effect, independence influences the snob effect, interdependence influences the bandwagon effect (Kastanakis & Balabanis, 2012).

In this chapter you will read about the influence of habitus and taste in fashion change. The theories that are discussed are reliant on judgments about "good" and "bad" and "appropriate" and "inappropriate." The Trickle Down theory examines how lower classes copied the styles of upper classes, while the Trickle Up theory examines how upper classes copied the styles of the lower classes. In both cases, as strata of society copy others, they engage in the process of fashion change. Dress scholar Evelyn Brannon (2005) called trickle up, trickle down, and trickle across directional theories. She explains, "The directional theories of fashion change make prediction easier by pointing to the likely starting points for a fashion trend, the expected direction that trend will take, and how long the trend will last" (p. 82). Additionally, this chapter will also examine social and economic motivations for acquiring styles by presenting the concept of scarcity/rarity, consumption theories and political motivations for adornment.

Trickle Down theory

The **Trickle Down** theory is a classic example of understanding how styles change. Conceived by sociologist George Simmel (1904), it is based on class structure and class difference. Sometimes you might hear it called "**Imitation/Differentiation**" or as anthropologist Grant McCracken (1988) called it, "**chase and flight**." All three of these names give us a good idea of what this theory espouses. The Trickle Down theory suggests that fashions begin in the upper-most class. The class directly beneath the upper-most class observes what the upper-most class is wearing and copies them. This is then repeated by subsequently lower classes, until people in most classes are wearing the same fashion. At this point the upper class does not want to wear what the lower classes are wearing and thus changes style, prompting the entire sequence to begin anew. This is a reflection of what McCracken called social distance, or using clothing to display one's social rank—and thereby social distance—from others. The imitation of the lower class by the upper class closes the social distance and the differentiation by the upper class re-establishes the social distance.

The Trickle Down theory is a classic understanding of fashion and was very relevant in societies that had strict class differences, such as Europe. In countries such as England, France, Germany, and Spain, people were divided into classes based on their heritage and pedigree during the Middle Ages. In general there were three classes: aristocracy, merchant, and working. Sometimes these could be split into further divisions, but in general kings and queens were at the apex, followed by nobles with titles such as prince, princess, duke, duchess, lord, lady, marquis, marchioness, baron, baroness, etc. The merchant class comprised business people who earned money and could be quite wealthy but did not have a title or noble pedigree. Nobles inherited wealth; merchants created wealth. The lowest level was the working class who worked as laborers or were peasants.

The king and queen of a land would wear a new style and it would be seen at court by the titled nobles. The titled nobles would copy what they saw, maybe because they liked the aesthetics or maybe because they wanted to curry favor from the king or queen and believed dressing like him or her would engender positive feelings, or maybe because they wanted to signal to others that they were in the same class as the king and queen. The merchants would then see what the titled nobles were wearing and copy what they saw, and would wear the style, which was then copied by their subordinates. By this time everyone in society was dressing like the king and queen, so they would have to alter their style in order to be different.

The Trickle Down theory explains the emergence of the three-piece suit. Its roots are traced to King Charles II of England in 1666. During this time in history the upper classes—especially the men—were very flamboyant in terms of their dress. Luxurious silks, laces, jewels, and fabrics made with gold and silver threads were not uncommon. It was a way to display one's wealth (see Conspicuous consumption, this chapter). Charles II was the first king after the Interregnum[1] and understood his situation was politically precarious; after all, his father King Charles I had been executed via beheading in a civil war between royal and Parliament rights and powers. To curb ostentatious display, he ordered his court to change their style of dress and offered a new outfit made of slacks, jacket, and vest "which he will never alter" (Pepys, 1972, p. 315). The phrase "never alter" references a standard suit immune from fashion trends. The fabric he chose was darkly-colored wool, and the cut of the suit was tailored. There was no ornamentation such as embroidery or gemstones; rather, the outfit was plain. He offered this as an option to reduce the *appearance* of excessive spending and encouraged his court to follow suit. He even wore it himself but eventually he and his court returned to their former ostentatious display of dress (Kuchta, 2007).

The idea of a somber, plain suit was picked up again by British Royalty during the Regency Period (1811–1820) when lush, expensive, flashy styles of dressing were eschewed for simplistic formality. Socialite and dandy Beau Brummel wore the simpler style, which was eventually adopted by others. Through the course of the next century, the suit was adopted as the basic and classic example of men's attire. Edward, the Duke of Windsor (1894–1972), also helped to popularize variations of the suit when he wore suits made of gray flannel or in the Glen plaid check (later renamed Prince of Wales check). Suits were adopted by men in professional executive positions and men seeking employment. Today suits are found at all price points, in many different fabrications, for many different customers, be they upper class or working class, have vast amounts of money or are on a budget. (Musgrave, 2009).

Sometimes, a king would enact a *sumptuary law*. **Sumptuary laws** were restrictions on the use of certain fabrics, materials, or adornments, according to class. Sumptuary laws were enacted at the time that merchant classes began to obtain wealth and could afford luxuries that heretofore could only be afforded by the nobility. They were designed to prevent (the "wrong") people from displaying wealth through clothing and are found in historical instances around the world. An ordinance from 1657 in the town of Nurnburg (today, Nuremberg, Germany) reads, "It is an unfortunately established fact that both men and women fold have, in utterly irresponsible manner, driven extravagance in dress and new style to such shameful and wanton extremes that the different classes are barely to be known apart" (Boehn, 1932–1935, III, 173). Sumptuary laws were found in Rome as early as 300 BC, in Colonial New England, Italy, Scotland, Spain, and England (Hunt, 1996). An interesting decree from 1669 Japan limits sumptuous costumes for puppets, except in the case of puppet generals (Shiveley, 1955).

Sumptuary laws were designed to control who could wear what status products. For example, Henry VIII enacted a sumptuary law in 1511 which restricted men's apparel by rank (women were exempt from this law); silver cloth, gold cloth, sable fur, and wool were restricted to the rank of lord and above; velvet was limited to men of knight rank and higher and was further restricted to color—blue or crimson only to those who held the rank of knight of the garter or higher; the decree also limited the amount of fabric a servant man could use in his dress (2½ yards) (Hooper, 1915). Historian Milla Davenport (1976) noted that sumptuary laws were often ineffective, repealed, or unenforceable. Thus, sumptuary laws did not necessarily deter people from engaging in trickle down fashion.

However, the Trickle Down theory did not only explain fashions in Medieval Europe. In the recent, modern era the story of the Teddy Boys is also the story of

Figure 3.2 The fashion of the Teddy Boys took cues from upper-class British society and the American Wild West. Joseph McKeown.

class differentiation and imitation. Beginning in 1950s London, the Teddy Boys were a group of working-class adolescents (see Figure 3.2). They worked jobs after school and had extra money in the pocket and chose to spend it on their appearance. They were inspired by, but did not adopt the exact dress of, the Edwardians.[2] Edwardian style, named for the reign of King Edward VII (r. 1901–1910), had a revival among the upper class after World War II. The Teddy Boys of the 1950s wore a mix of British Edwardian style and American West style. From the original Edwardians they adopted drape jackets and slim "drainpipe" pants and from the American West they adopted vests and slim bowties. Their clothes, however, were generally made from luxury fabrications such as wool, brocade, and velvet which was incongruent with the occupations of working-class men. It was perceived as pretentious and socially rebellious. Additionally, the somewhat unsavory habits of the Teddy Boys got them labeled as gangs in the media. Consequently, the Edwardian style was no longer desired by the upper and middle classes in England who turned to other forms of dress.

Notions of class have often differed between Europe and the United States. In Europe class is based on pedigree and being born into a class, and often, one could not change one's class. In the United States, class is based on money, not birth, and a person could change one's class with financial success and learning social skills relevant to the aspired class. However, it appears that traditional notions of class have changed in both the United States and Britain. Since Margaret Thatcher's election to the role of Prime Minister in 1979, the British class system started to change: "Money, which has not really featured in the British demarcation of social class, became very important. . . . As Thatcher was working to open things up and making the British class system more like America's, the US class system started becoming more rigid" (Goldfarb, 2013, n.p.). Meanwhile, in the United States, the class system shifted from one of money to one of heritage. With regard to the Trickle Down theory of fashion this implies a shift who originates a trend today—those with money or those with pedigree?

The Trickle Down theory is about visually achieving status through clothing and appearance and the actual item that conveys status need not be expensive, just worn by the upper class. However, that item needs to be exclusive to the originating class at least for the time being (Brannon, 2005). Originally, the Trickle Down theory explained fashion change in Europe and America in the modern period until the middle of the 20th century, when social structure was based on class. McCracken (1988) observed that the social system is actually more layers than originally conceived by Simmel, and Kaiser (1990) noted today's society has a hierarchy of layers conceived of demographics other than class/wealth: gender, race, age, and attractiveness. To this one could add fame, notoriety, sexual orientation, ethnicity, skin color/tone, and power. Additionally, fashion scholar Jennifer Craik (1994) argued, "Everyday fashion . . . does not simply 'trickle down' from the dictates of the self-proclaimed elite. At best, a particular mode may tap into everyday sensibilities and be popularised" (p. ix). Thus, the process today is more complex than simple "cut and paste" from higher to lower classes.

61

As the postmodern era began, the Trickle Down theory no longer adequately explained fashion change. Fashion styles were now originating from the common man as worn on the street. An alternative to the Trickle Down theory is the **Trickle Up** theory which explained this new phenomenon: fashions start in the lowest classes and are adopted by higher and higher classes until they reach the top class. This theory was proffered by scholar George Field (1970) and he called it "the status float phenomenon." Anthropologist Ted Polhemus (1994) called it "bubble up."

Fashion scholar Dorothy Behling (1985/1986) suggested that the direction of fashion—trickle up or trickle down—is determined by the median age of the population. She argued that role models will evolve from a population's median age. When the median age is older, role models will likely be from upper classes and fashions will trickle down. However, when the median age is younger, role models will come from the lower classes, likely have little money, and therefore fashion will trickle up.

The A-shirt or singlet or tank top undershirt (sometimes disrespectfully referred to in the colloquial as "wifebeater") is a white, sleeveless shirt usually made from ribbed, knit, cotton fabric. Its origins as an undershirt helped men remain dry when it was worn with dress shirts. However, working class men wore it without an outer shirt. Old School Hip Hop also adopted the shirt and helped to disseminate the style to a different market and designers like Calvin Klein offered luxe versions made from smooth cotton weaves in black. However, some people question the taste of wearing them. A recent examination of thread in an Internet chartroom asked the question: "Are 'wife beaters' low class?" The overwhelming majority of response was in the affirmative. One person wrote, "They remind me of some guy from a 40s movie who lives in a fleabag apartment, smokes a short cigar, and yes, smacks his wife" (GalileoSmith, 2010). Others complained about the appearance of underarm hair as a sign of their low class status. However, a minority of people who posted on the thread said they were permissible under specific conditions—if the underarm hair was shaven, the man wearing it was muscular, or if worn by toned, athletic women. Nonetheless, despite their working class origins, they have at times been fashionable regardless of the question of taste.

Like the origins of the fashionable A-shirt, jeans have a working-class pedigree as well. Levi Strauss was an immigrant who arrived in California in 1853 and opened a wholesale dry goods business in San Francisco. One of his clients was another immigrant, Jacob Davis, who found a way to improve workers' pants durability by using copper rivets at the stress points. However, he did not have the financial capital to patent the idea so he explained this concept to Strauss and the two became partners. On May 20, 1873 they were granted a patent for "improvement in fastening pocket-openings" (*Pacific Rural Press*, June 28, 1873, p. 406). Strauss and Davis began to manufacture riveted work pants using denim imported from New Hampshire (Downey, 2009). The pants were originally known as "overalls" or

Figure 3.3 Before Levi Strauss denim jeans became fashionable, they were the work wear of laborers, such as these miners in 1882. Courtesy Levi Strauss & Co. Archives, San Francisco.

"waist overalls" because they were designed as protective clothing to be worn over one's regular clothing while working (see Figure 3.3). It was not until the early 20th century that their function transitioned to being worn as street clothing itself.

Jeans reached another market during World War II when factory workers wore them. The durability and strength of the pants were complimentary to the hard labor in machine shops and factories. But it was not until the 1950s that jeans started to gain popularity and were worn as a fashion statement. In the 1950s "teenagers" had become a new market when high school students who worked after school began to earn spending money. Teenagers were also rebellious against the status quo and turned to jeans as an alternative to the "proper attire" they were expected to wear. It also did not hurt that anti-hero actor James Dean wore jeans in the highly popular film *Rebel Without A Cause* (1955) as did other actors in similarly themed films, such as Marlon Brando in *The Wild One* (1953) and Dennis Hopper and Peter Fonda in the film *Easy Rider* (1969). Wearing them was considered inappropriate for the middle and upper classes because the originated from the working class. They were not refined like the woolen slacks that were common among middle class and upper class people. Plus, they had a bad reputation, given their association with subcultures that also adopted jeans, like Greasers and Hippies. They came to symbolize the anti-establishment.

In the mid-1970s heiress and designer Gloria Vanderbilt offered a line of fashionable and high quality women's jeans. This brought the aforementioned "bad taste" jeans to a new market, but this time the garment was marketed as glamorous. Through the 1980s and 1990s the business of jeans increased dramatically and slowly made inroads into accepted fashion. Likely the advent of "Casual Fridays" (see Chapter 4) also helped society's adoption of jeans and changed perceptions about them. By the end of the 20th century other designers were offering jeans in their collections and luxury houses such as Prada, Armani, and Dior were doing the same. Today, jeans are ubiquitous and are common staples of one's wardrobe from people working in low-paying jobs in factories and on farms to high-paying executives of Fortune 500 companies.

Coco Chanel also looked to the working class for inspiration with her designs. More on Chanel's design aesthetic is discussed in Chapter 4 but at least one of her iconic designs were appropriated from the dress of the working class. The little black dress was a modification of the shop girl, maid, or nun's uniform, depending on your perspective and source of information. However, her creations were made with panache and she elevated them to fashion. Wilson (2003) notes that Chanel's "[little] black dress and slight suit were the apotheosis of the shop girl's uniform, or the stenographer's garb" (p. 41). Chanel's use of the working class for inspiration exemplifies the Trickle Up theory. Until Chanel, shop girls and secretaries were not considered fashionable. Fashion theorist Catherine Driscoll (2010) noted that Chanel's "poor look" was akin to anti-fashion and disrupted the usual phenomenon of fashion originating from the upper classes. This time fashion rose from below.

Scarcity/Rarity

The concept of scarcity or rarity is noteworthy in the fashion industry because for many people it is the elusive or unusual or different that they seek in their dress. Products in limited supply give their owners prestige and status because not everyone can own the product. That there is a dearth of products to be distributed to everyone means that those who can attain those products are "special," because they have the resources or access to the items. Note how this relates to uniqueness as discussed in Chapter 2.

Some items are in limited supply due to nature. Many gemstones and precious metals are considered rare because they are difficult to find/mine or because only a small amount of them exist in the world. Platinum, gold, and silver have long been viewed as prestigious metals because of their relatively rare state. Gems such as emeralds, rubies, and sapphires are commonly known and can be found in most jewelry stores, but gemstones such as red diamonds, painite, green garnet, blue garnet, red beryl, and poudretteite are so rare that only a handful of each are known to exist.

Other items are naturally abundant but their scarcity is manufactured by humans. Diamonds are such a case (see Figure 3.4). In nature, white diamonds are plentiful, but due to the monopolistic maneuverings of diamond conglomerate DeBeers, the company was able to control the supply of diamonds. They set prices, limited market availability and produced clever marketing campaigns to make consumers believe that ownership of a diamond was special because they were "rare" (Kanfer, 1993). The myth still persists today.

And still other items are manufactured purposefully in limited supply. Hermès Birkin bags have historically been in short supply. Not only did interested consumers need to spend upwards of US$10,000 for a basic model but they also were on a waiting list for years until their order was delivered. The combination of price and time meant that very few people could own the bag. Today the waiting list has been eliminated but the bag still retains its aurora of exclusivity. Other companies have followed this format and produce limited editions of popular products. Armani

Figure 3.4 This bracelet is considered valuable because it is made with diamonds which are in limited supply in the market. The limited supply is not natural but manufactured by industry practices. Bracelet courtesy of Marcia Morgado/image by Attila Pohlmann.

65

hired singer Rihanna to design lingerie for Emporio Armani in 2011, and TOMS and Nike manufacture limited edition shoes regularly. Likewise, Prada only produces a few of its runway pieces and disperses them to its retail outlets around the globe. At a 2011 trunk show for Prada in Honolulu, three men arrived wearing the same sparkly green shirt. When asked about their shirts, a customer replied that Prada only made 50 and "three of them are here in room now." Whereas in many cases wearing the same item as another person would be social death, in this case the exclusivity and rarity of the sparkly green shirts signaled to "those in the know" the special status of the wearers.

Yet, businesses have violated the rule of exclusivity in order to increase profits and reach a larger market-share. The results had been near catastrophe for one, and the end of a lucrative business for another. For example, Gucci products were highly valued in the 1960s. The workmanship, design, and quality of leathers and hardware made Gucci handbags and shoes highly desirable. Owning a Gucci item indicated that the possessor was not only stylish but also affluent, for Gucci products were very expensive. Consumers would even deal with rude salespeople or inconvenient shopping hours to own a Gucci product (Forden, 2001). In the 1970s, due to a tangle of Gucci-family politics and business ventures, the company began selling inexpensive canvas bags printed with the iconic Gucci logo (Forden, 2001). These were eagerly bought by people who until then could only dream of owning something from Gucci. The unintended result was that the Gucci brand was devalued. Once anyone could own a Gucci item it made ownership less special. The customers who had always purchased expensive Gucci products stopped buying—why buy when anyone can? The Gucci executives eventually saw the error of their thinking, ceased production on the cheap canvas bags, and took measures to reclaim their status as luxury icon. Gucci violated the rule of exclusivity and rarity in diversifying its product mix to include cheap goods.

Another example of flawed business decision that did not take into account exclusivity or prestige of the brand was Halston (see Figure 3.5). Throughout the 1970s Halston was the auteur of chic American design. He designed matching separates in single colors and elegant gowns. A First Lady and numerous movie stars and socialites wore Halston designs. Jacqueline Kennedy wore his pill-box hats. Bianca Jagger, Liza Minelli, Barbara Walters, and Liz Taylor were just a few of his celebrity clients. He—and his creations—were regulars at the star-studded club of its time, Studio 54 in New York City, and it seemed everyone wanted to be draped in Halston. His line was carried by luxury retailer Bergdorf-Goodman. Then, in 1982 Halston sold his name to mid-range retailer J. C. Penney. Bergdorf-Goodman stopped carrying the Halston label because Halston designs could now be found at the mid-price-range American department store. Halston also licensed his name to fragrances, luggage, and carpets. The Halston brand had become overexposed and associated with the middle class. No one wanted to wear Halston anymore. The Halston name—once synonymous with glamour and wealth—was now synonymous with shopping malls and clearance sales. The aura of this exclusive fashion had

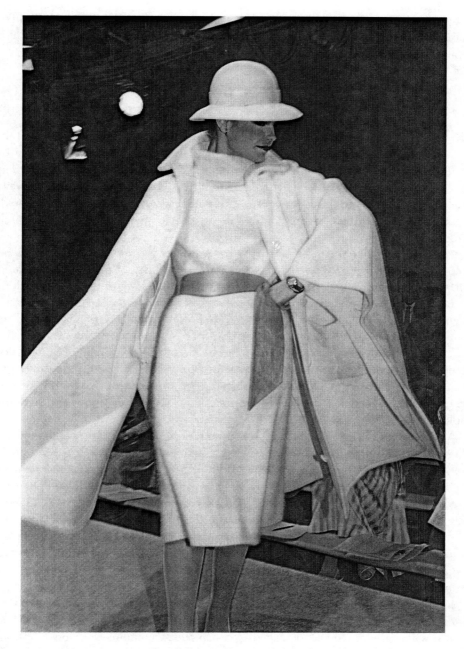

Figure 3.5 The Halston brand lost value when Halston III for J. C. Penney was offered to consumers. Although this seemed like a good business plan to extend the brand into a new market, many consumers felt it devalued the Halston reputation. Tony Palmieri/WWD © Condé Nast 1984.

disappeared. Roy Halston tried to revive his brand but passed away in 1990. Like the Gucci example, overexposure and mass diversifying of the brand resulted in a weaker consumer demand.

Conspicuous consumption

The theory of conspicuous consumption finds its origins in sociologist Thorstein Veblen's *A Theory of the Leisure Class* (1899). He articulated that at the top of society were the leisure class, people whose inherited (or made) wealth afforded the luxury of a life of leisure. He articulated that this class of people visually conveys their status through purchases (or consumption) that were obvious (or conspicuous). With matters of dress, people adorned themselves with expensive apparel, accessories, and fragrances.

In order for this theory to "work" the products people purchase must be recognized as having some type of value, be it the cost, rarity, or the status associated with owning the product. We see this often in the purchasing of rare goods such as precious gems and metals or in the purchase of luxury branded products from Chanel, Prada, Dior, Christian Louboutin, Tom Ford, Armani, Hermès, Escada, Etro, Louis Vuitton, etc. (see Figure 3.6). Such purchases are often not necessary or functional (a white shirt is a white shirt) but by virtue of being branded by a luxury company increase their prestige (a white shirt from Gap sends a different message than a white shirt from Dolce & Gabbana). The meaning or symbolism of the product takes precedence over its actual function, though function is still relevant (Solomon & Rabolt, 2004).

A **fetish** is an object believed to have supernatural or mystical power. Examples of fetishes are often found in religion, such as Christianity's holy water, the Voodoo's doll, or Native American's totems. Ethnologist John Ferguson McLennan (1896/1870) argued that this results in a relationship between people and material goods rather than people and their god. Psychologist Sigmund Freud (1995) extended the concept to sexual behavior and described a fetish as a substitution. Economist and philosopher Karl Marx used this concept to conceive a theory he called **commodity fetishism**. Very simply put, in a society where commodities are given perceived value, social relationships are based on the perceived value or cost of their commodities.

McCracken (1988) wrote that current consumer culture as we know it today owes much to the transformation in consumption to Elizabethan England (1558–1603), where the aristocracy engaged in conspicuous spending and consumption. He writes, "Elizabethan nobleman entertained one another, their subordinates, and, occasionally, their monarch at ruinous expense. A favorite device was the ante-supper. Guests sat down to this vast banquet only to have it removed, dispensed with, and replaced by a still more extravagant meal. Clothing was equally magnificent in character and expense" (p. 11). McCracken identified two reasons for this

Figure 3.6 Luxury designer brands, like Louis Vuitton, offer people the opportunity to conspicuously display their wealth through products that are recognized as being expensive. Greg Ward NZ/Shutterstock.com.

unprecedented and historic consumption of luxurious goods. First, it was a way for Elizabeth I to consolidate power by forcing her nobility to come to her to ask for resources. Second, the atmosphere at the Elizabethan court encouraged the nobility to compete with each other for the queen's attention and her favor. By the 18th century, merchants were engaging in marketing, more goods were available for consumption, and the pace of fashion change had increased. By the 19th century, the development of the department store as a source for one-stop shopping also brought with it a type of entertainment through its visual merchandising and architectural design; it was also a fashionable place to see and be seen.

McCracken's account of Elizabethan England's consumption was not the first instance of conspicuous consumption. Evidence exists of conspicuous consumption in the ancient world. In an often repeated story, legend has it that Cleopatra and Mark Antony made a wager to see who could create the most expensive meal. Mark Antony's menu no doubt dazzled Cleopatra, but her dish trumped his. At this time in Egyptian history, pearls were highly prized and very expensive. Cleopatra took a large pearl, dissolved it in a glass of wine, and drank it. Cleopatra won the wager. Evidence also exists of conspicuous consumption in ancient Rome where purple fabric was given status because of its relatively expensive and difficult procurement process. Divers had to explore dangerous waters to find the special mollusc whose ink was used as the dye base for the color purple. Finding enough molluscs was a costly process as many divers had to be employed. Wearing purple subsequently became synonymous with the upper class.

Conspicuous consumption has therefore existed for two millennia if not longer, but in recent decades, production time to produce goods has decreased dramatically. "From 1971, when Nike sold its first shoe, to 1989, the average lifespan of its shoe designs decreased from seven years to ten months. Constant innovation in shoe design compels customers to keep up with fashion and buy shoes more frequently" (Skoggard, 1998, p. 59). This means that new styles of a product are offered (and consumed) much more quickly today than in past decades, thus making recent styles "old" or "outdated" and in order for people to continually display their status they need to purchase products more frequently than before.

Yet, one need not be wealthy to engage in conspicuous consumption. The appearance of wealth can be created through the use of credit cards or spending exorbitantly in one area while neglecting others. In addition, many wealthy people are not necessarily engaging in conspicuous consumption today. Business theorists Thomas J. Stanley and William Danko (1996) examined consumption and income and divided people into two groups: under accumulators of wealth and prodigious accumulators of wealth. They found that prodigious accumulators (or wealthy people) are more likely to conserve money and live a frugal lifestyle. Conversely, under accumulators spend more money on status goods to create a façade of wealth.

There are two slight variations to the classic Conspicuous Consumption theory, status consumption and invidious consumption. Below, the differences are noted.

Conspicuous Consumption: purchasing products that obviously display status or wealth. For example, buying and using a Chanel purse to show (perceived) economic ability or resources to your friends, as described above.

Status Consumption: purchasing products that assist with group acceptance. Contrary to conspicuous consumption, these products may not necessarily be obvious but rather are used by people to fit into different social situations (O'Cass & McEwen, 2004, 34). For example, buying and using a Chanel purse to be accepted as "one of us" by a circle of friends.

Invidious Consumption: making purchases for the sake of invoking envy in others (Veblen, 1899). For example, buying a Chanel purse to make your friends jealous.

Conspicuous consumption is often perceived as vulgar, gaudy, and lacking taste. However, in the 1990s a new fashion for wearing simplified cuts and plain designs was noted (see Chapter 2, p. 38, "Aesthetic perception and learning", an example of refined aesthetics in the 1990s). Fashion scholar Rebecca Arnold (2000)'s assessment of the new style was that it was "**Inconspicuous consumption**: wearing clothes whose very simplicity betrays their expense and cultural value, when quiet, restrained luxury is still revered as the ultimate symbol of both wealth and intelligence" (p. 169). Only a person "in the know" will know.

Political use of fashion

Because fashion is semiotic and can carry meaning, the dress of people can carry political overtones, especially when they are seeking to disrupt or change the status quo. In the United States red and blue colors carry political dimensions; red is aligned with the Republican party and blue with the Democratic party. Congressional senators and representatives often wear the color of their party during campaigns. As part of the Chinese Cultural Revolution (1966–1976), leader Mao Zedong outlawed silk and ornamentation, which he viewed as elitist and capitalistic, and instituted a unisex jacket and pants combination that became known as the Mao Suit. During the reign of Queen Victoria of the United Kingdom (1837–1901), she decreed that Scottish men sew the side of their kilts to avoid any immodesty; many men, however, saw this as an attack on Scottish nationality and refused to do so as a political protest. During the Indian move for independence from the United Kingdom in the early 20th century, Mahatma Gandhi advocated for his supporters to adopt locally-made kahdi fabric rather than British fabrics.

There are political considerations about what nation's clothing is worn. When John F. Kennedy was campaigning for the United States presidency in the 1960s, his wife, status icon Jacqueline Bouvier Kennedy, was criticized for wearing French designers. Since then, First Ladies and potential First Ladies have worn American designers and branded clothes, like Nancy Regan's red Aldofo suits, or Michelle Obama's choice of Jason Wu for inaugural gowns and J. Crew for daywear. Similarly,

British Prime Minister Tony Blair abandoned Italian suits for British suits during his political career (Gaulme & Gaulme, 2012).

There are political considerations about where apparel is manufactured. Apparel made offshore tends to be cheaper but at a cost to manufacturing in jobs in the home country. For example, China has become one of the leaders of mass-produced manufacturing, with an industry built around cheap labor. However, some people view the outsourcing of labor from one country to another as problematic. The practices of some countries tend to raise concerns about sweatshops and unfair labor issues. Issues include forced labor, little pay, hazardous conditions, no overtime, long hours, and no breaks. This ethical issue has led to boycotts of clothing produced in foreign countries and "buy local" campaigns, but efforts may be undermined by shady regulations and practices. Saipan is an island in the Pacific Ocean where these types of conditions are found, but because it is a territory of the United States, clothing is labeled "Made in the USA," misleading consumers trying to make ethically-sound purchases.

The two following examples illustrate how pants have had political connotations during two different historic occasions. During the French Revolution, the Sans Culottes distinctive dress style was associated with violence in the name of government reform. In the United States, the bloomer outfit became associated with women's rights. Both fashions existed for a short, specific period of time and both demonstrate how clothing can be linked to political movements.

Sans Culottes

In the 1780s in France, fashion took on political overtones that threatened the health and safety (literally) of the ruling aristocracy. The fashionable mode at the time for those who could afford it was Rococo, a style known for its excess in everything from fabrics to jewelry. Those who were opposed to the royalist government looked to ancient Rome for inspiration. The classical Roman Republic (509 BC–27 BC) was viewed as the ideal form of government by the people for the people. The robe à la française, a sack gown featuring Watteau pleats at the back neck, and the robe à l'anglaise, an ensemble of fitted bodice and wide skirt, were the mode of the French royal court and its followers. But, opponents of the court wore loose neo-classical chemises of supple fabrics, inspired by Classical Rome.

A group of working class men, however, opted for a different mode of dress, one that was sartorially different from the ruling elite to express their political position. The style became known as the Sans Culottes and was adopted 1792–1794. The Sans Culottes were a political organization who advocated democratic rule and supported the left-wing government entities that ruled France during the Revolution via building barricades and providing support for violent attacks and massacres. Sans Culottes translates as "without culottes" and was originally a disparaging term that indicated the person was lower class. At the time the wealthy merchant class and aristocracy wore culottes (or breeches) usually made of expensive fabrics like

Figure 3.7 The Sans Culottes of the French Revolution were politically motivated to change social structure and identified by their clothing, especially their pants, short jacket and red cap. Mark Hamilton.

silk. Sans Culottes, rather, wore pants. The Phrygian cap, also known as the liberty cap, was a red hat that was worn by slaves in Classical Rome and was adopted as symbolic headgear. In addition they sometimes wore the short-skirted coat known as the carmagnole and clogs. However, not all apparel items need to be worn together to be considered a Sans Culottes.

During the Terror, clothing of the middle class and aristocracy "served as evidence of guilt. Silk, lace, jewels, or any form of metal embroidery was a sign of the *ancien régime*, as were hair powder, wigs, or any elaborate form of coiffure. Even good grooming and cleanliness became suspect" (North, 2008, 190). Some people started to wear the Sans Culottes style as a means to avoid injury. The Terror ended with the Thermidorian Reaction when leaders of the Terror were executed. As a result the Sans Culottes no longer had government support and eventually disbanded.

Bloomers

The events that occurred in the 19th century Antebellum South (United States) related to changing the way women dressed and what they wore became collectively known as the Dress Reform Movement. In actuality it was a lot of small movements by different groups of people with different motivations for changing dress. Health and gender equality were frequently cited as reasons for reform. The weight of undergarments and the constricting nature of corsets were often cited as health issues. In the 1850s women were wearing as many as 12 layers of clothing (Fischer, 2001) which was putting a great strain on women's waists and torsos. Corsets and tight-lacing reduced women's waists to numbers in the teens (e.g., 13–19 inches) which resulted in internal organs being displaced and compacted. Pantaloons were also apparel garments cited for change. "Pantaloons dress reformers . . . wanted to reform female dress for comfortable fit, physical well-being, religious beliefs, women's rights, or work opportunities—not to blur the distinction between the sexes" (2001, p. 83).

Fischer (2001) noted that it was first in 1827, in the utopian community of New Harmony, that "the connection between pantaloons and gender equality [had] been forged and would become the most important themes in dress to symbolize equality" (p. 38). Pantaloons did not become popular but resurfaced in 1848 in another utopian community, Oneida. However, they were seldom worn in private, mostly worn in public. Three years later in 1851 three women would wear them in public in Seneca Falls, New York: Elizabeth Smith Miller, Elizabeth Cody Stanton, and Amelia Jenks Bloomer.

What became known as "bloomers" and erroneously attributed to Amelia Jenks Bloomer's creative imagination, was actually created by Elizabeth Smith Miller. Elizabeth Smith Miller designed a set of matching pants and short skirt (short for the time, mid-calf). Her friend Elizabeth Cody Stanton copied the design, as did Amelia Jenks Bloomer. Their new style of clothing was adopted by other dress reformers. Miller, Stanton, and Bloomer argued that the new style was healthier but did not link it to gender equality, because they realized that health was a stronger platform for change (Fischer, 2001). Nonetheless, bloomers were viewed as a fight for gender equality, while proponents saw them as a fight for men's power. Women who wore bloomers, like Susan B. Antony, were ridiculed and harassed. The press did not help either and produced harsh commentaries and critiques about the women who wore them. Many who wore the garment were seen as trying to subvert men's power. Around 1854 dress reformers started to discard the style, though Amelia Jenks Bloomer continued to wear them until 1858 (Fischer, 2001). Although the bloomer did not reach a national level, it nonetheless constitutes a fashion among a very specific group of people that had political motivations and overtones.

BOXED CASE 3.1: CINDERELLA'S GLASS SLIPPER

Have you ever wondered why Cinderella's shoe was made of glass? Regardless of whether a glass slipper could actually be made, why was her footwear for the royal ball not made of decadent silk or sumptuous velvet? Why glass? Cultural historian Kathryn A. Hoffmann offers a convincing explanation for this meme. The following summation is based on a presentation Hoffmann gave at the "Cenerentola come Testo Culturale/Cinderalla as a Text of Culture" conference in Rome in November 2012.

Stories of a poor, destitute girl who meets her Prince Charming and lives happily ever after are found where the footwear varies from sandal to golden shoe to red velour mule, but it is Perrault's version of "Cendrillon" with the glass slipper that most people recognize. Charles Perrault was a 17th century French author who penned some of the well-known versions of fairy tales still read today. It was Perrault who gave the heroine a slipper of glass.

In 17th century France, glass was a desired commodity and examples of ornate, decorative, and decadent glass products, from tables to mirrors to sculptures abounded in palaces and homes. The desire for imported glass from Venice even resulted in an outpouring of money from France, espionage related to the procurement of glass, and a few poisonings in which international plots were suspected. Sabine Melchior-Bonnet recounts some of that history in *The Mirror: A History*. Hoffmann argued that "Perrault's glass slipper appeared in a line of fairy tales with glass elements and at the time of what can only be described as a French mania for glass."

But the selection of glass as the material for Cinderella's slipper was not arbitrary or based solely on the fashion of the moment. Rather, glass was featured in Italian and French fairy tales and was laden with sexuality and death: glass caskets, a glass tunnel, and fairy palaces of glass and crystal. Hoffmann noted, "Glass fits the patterns of both death (the forgotten girl among the cinders) and magical sexuality."

Thus, we can interpret the glass slipper in a few ways. At the time of Perrault's writing, glass was highly fashionable; therefore the glass slipper is the mode. Also at the time of Perrault's writing, glass was expensive and linked to wealth and royalty; therefore the glass slipper is a sign of status. Also, prior fairy tales linked glass to sexuality; therefore the glass slipper represents femininity. Whatever your interpretation, this notion of a glass slipper has prevailed and been offered in different shoe iterations, including those made of Plexiglas, vinyl, or covered in rhinestones.

BOXED CASE 3.2: ETHICS FOCUS: THE DIAMOND MONOPOLY

Popular thought is that diamonds are rare. Their seemingly limited supply is one reason why they fetch high fees per carat. However, in actuality, diamonds are not scarce—they are made of carbon, one of the most plentiful elements on earth—and the myth of their rarity was created by diamond conglomerate DeBeers.

In the 1870s business man Cecil Rhodes began buying tracts of lands in present-day Kimberly, South Africa, on which diamonds had been discovered. Under Rhodes and later Ernst Oppenheimer, DeBeers (named after the owners of one of the land tracts) became the largest diamond company in the world and established a network that controlled price and flow of diamonds onto the markets. Their practices included quashing competition, buying competitive diamond mines to shut them down, stockpiling diamonds, and refusing to sell diamonds to people outside their network (Kanfer, 1993). Then, through a clever "diamonds are forever" advertising campaign, consumers began to view diamonds as heirlooms and rare, thus keeping them forever and not reselling them (Kanfer, 1993). The monopoly ended in the early 21st century when conflict diamonds (diamonds mined to support wars) became a moral issue and consumers started buying other gemstones. Nonetheless, DeBeers remains one of the largest and most profitable diamond suppliers in the world.

DeBeers' practices, by restricting what diamond suppliers and designers and cutters can purchase diamonds, created an artificial scarcity. Because they marketed diamonds as valuable, keepsakes, and symbols of love and marriage, they created a desire among people for them. As a result, diamonds were used as conspicuous consumption. Their status as "rare" and expensive makes them a luxury item where size and quality were indicators of wealth and class. Consequently, consumers were (and still are) willing to pay enormous amounts for shiny bits of hardened carbon.

Summary

At the social level, fashion is influenced by habitus and taste that includes and excludes people based on their manner of dress. One of the first theories to explain fashion change, the Trickle Down theory was based on social structure; a number of theories since then have looked at fashion through the lens of society. When there was a paradigm shift in the mid-20th century, the direction of fashion influence reversed with styles originating in the street and working their way up through higher echelons of society. While other theories have also explained how trends move through social strata, the need to display one's class (or assume the aesthetics of another's class) is common among them all.

Key Terms

- Bandwagon effect
- Chase and flight
- Commodity fetishism
- Conspicuous consumption
- Fetish
- Habitus
- Imitation/differentiation
- Inconspicuous consumption

- Invidious consumption
- Snob effect
- Status consumption
- Taste
- Trickle down
- Trickle up
- Sumptuary Laws
- Veblen effect

Discussion questions

1. If people like to possess exclusive or rare items why do not more brands offer limited edition products? What qualities make "limited edition" valuable?
2. Identify a product you bought where your motivation was to display (perceived) wealth, incite envy, or to fit in with a group of people.
3. List 5–10 items of the lower/working class that have become fashionable. List 5–10 that have not. Why do you think some became fashionable while others did not?
4. Simmel conceived the social system having upper class and lower class. Kaiser added gender, race, age and attractiveness as other strata of social organization. It was also suggested that fame, notoriety, sexual orientation, ethnicity, skin color/tone, and power are possible alternatives to social strata. Are there any forms of social organization that you would add?

Learning activities

1. Examine ads in fashion magazines and categorize them according to one of the three consumption theories discussed.
2. Show people an A-shirt and conduct a brief interview. Ask them to comment on it. Who wears it? Where do they wear it? Why do they wear it? Is it considered low class? Is it fashion? Organize their responses by theme. Do the themes tell you anything about taste? If the people you interviewed differ by age, is there a difference between older people and younger people?
3. Find a location where you can observe people, like a coffee shop or a bench in a park. As people walk by, analyze their mode of dress. How many scarce or rare items do you see? How many of these items are truly rare and how many are rare by human influence? Interpret your findings to relate to social organization.

Notes

1. The period in British History when England was ruled by Oliver Cromwell, after Charles I (Charles II's father) was executed; 1649–1660.
2. Ted is a nickname for Edward.

Further reading

Davis, F. (1989). Of blue jeans and maids' uniforms: The drama of status ambivalences in clothing and fashion. *Qualitative Sociology, 12* (4), 337–355.

Kanfer, S. (1993). *The Last Empire: DeBeers, Diamonds, and the World*. London: Hodder and Stoughton.

Korotchenko, A., & Clarke, L. H. (2010). Russian immigrant women and the negotiation of social class and feminine identity through fashion. *Critical Studies in Fashion and Beauty, 1* (2), pp. 181–202.

Morgado, M. (2003). From kitsch to chic: The transformation of Hawaiian shirt aesthetics. *Clothing and Textiles Research Journal, 21* (2), 75–88.

Paulicelli, E. (2004). *Fashion Under Fascism: Beyond the Black Shirt*. Oxford: Berg.

Skoggard, I. (1989). Transnational commodity flows and the global phenomenon of the brand. In A. Brydon & S. Niessen (eds) *Consuming Fashion: Adorning the Transnational Body* (pp. 57–70.) Oxford: Berg.

Trigg, A. B. (2001). Veblen, Bourdieu and conspicuous consumption. *Journal of Economic Issues, 35* (1), 99–115.

4

FASHION AND CULTURE

A culture must be open to new ideas, experimentation, and social mobility for fashion to exist. Fashion cannot exist in a culture where people submit their will to a higher order. Some religious orders require their members to show their devotion by wearing specific dress: the Anabaptists (Amish, Brethren, Hutterites, and Mennonites; see Figure 4.1) wear plain dress (dress sans decoration) that does not change season to season (Druesedow, 2010). Some governments require their subjects to wear particular dress to show their allegiance: leaders of Nazi Germany prescribed uniforms and dress codes for its people (Guenther, 2004). Such cultures do not support a fashion system because fashion is about *change* and (sometimes) about individual expression.

After World War II, when Germany was divided into West and East, fashion flourished in West Germany because it was a free-economy and a free culture where people were allowed to decide for themselves how to dress and what to wear. However, across the border, East Germany was a socialist country with alliances tied to the communist-controlled Soviet Union. In theory, socialist and communist societies advocate equality of everyone, everyone is given what they need to live, and all people are treated equally. In a socialist or communist society, all people earn the same salary regardless of their profession—because they are contributing to the prosperity of the nation—and the government in turn provides people with their needs, such as transportation, food, and clothing. Notice the word here is clothing, not fashion. Socialist and communist governments tend to consider fashion to be consumerist, elitist, and wasteful. In East Germany the government wanted to regulate production and consumption of clothing (Stitziel, 2005). In theory, all raw materials were to be supplied by the state and the design, manufacture, and distribution of clothing was governed by the state. In East Germany, prototypes of clothing were developed to make choices simpler for manufacturers and ultimately for the consumers. However, in reality, people refused to purchase clothing offered to them because they did not like the style or fabrications. Another result was that everyone ended up looking the same (good if you want to visually illustrate the unity of a people, but bad if you want to communicate individuality). People who

Figure 4.1 The Amish wear traditional clothes that do not change style from season to season. Their dress reflects a religious devotion expressed by a plain countenance. Julie Whitehead.

desired to look different were often at risk of arrest, interrogation, and imprisonment (Wilms, 2009). In the end, the experiment with planned production of clothing was a failure and when the government fell in 1989 a free-market economy replaced the planned economy.

Fashion needs capitalism or free-exchange in order to survive (Sproles & Burns, 1994; Kaiser, Nagasawa & Hutton, 1995). Consumers must be allowed to make choices when dressing themselves, though seldom are their choices unaffected by outside influences. In this chapter you will read about the connection between culture and fashion: how fashion is a reflection of the times; how cultures exchange aesthetic ideas that influence fashion; how fashion moves from city to city; why some groups of people are inspirations for fashions; and how fashion reflects a division between old and new.

Zeitgeist

Sociologist Herbert Blumer (1969) coined the term **Zeitgeist** to explain how fashions are a product of the times in which they were developed and worn. Zeitgeist is a German word meaning "spirit of the times" (Zeit = times, geist = spirit). Marketing professor Paul Nystrom (1929) identified five areas that represent the Zeitgeist: dominating events, dominating ideals, dominating social groups, dominating attitudes, and dominating technology. As fashion and style are representative of events, ideals, groups, attitudes, and technology, fashion itself becomes a reflection of the Zeitgeist. This explains why a style becomes popular in a given time and is linked to a specific era.

When World War II ended, Christian Dior sought to open his own fashion house. He already had experience before the war with fashion designers Robert Piguet and Lucien Lelong but he did not have the financing to start a business. He asked textile entrepreneur Marcel Boussac to finance his business. Boussac agreed but required Dior to use lots of material and buy the material from his textile manufacturers. Dior agreed but had the dilemma of designing aesthetically pleasing clothing using as much fabric as possible. Fortunately for him, at this time in Paris was an exhibition of the Belle Époque. The Belle Époque—translated from the French as *beautiful era*—occurred at the end of the 19th century and beginning of the 20th century when fashion was elegant, feminine, and used lots of fabric. *Voila*! Dior had his inspiration. But it would not be enough for Dior to design beautiful clothing; his customers had to want to wear them—and they did. For the prior two decades women were used to wearing clothing with slim silhouettes because of fabric shortages and streamlined clothing was necessary when working in factories during wartime. They were ready for a change from their masculine-tailored suits and dresses and when Dior showed his first collection of voluminous, full silhouettes, they embraced a return to feminine clothing. The then editor-in-chief of *Harper's Bazaar*, Carmel Snow, said Christian Dior had created a "new look" for women (see Figure 4.2). That sobriquet stuck and identified a whole era of fashion.

This example represents the connection between fashion and the Zeitgeist. By examining the spirit of the times, it explains how fashion was a reflection of the "moment" or "era." It combines economics (Dior wanted to open a fashion show, Boussac had funding provided he use textiles bought from his firms), history (Dior looked to the past to create his collection) and social-psychology (women were ready for a change in the way they dressed).

Today we see the Zeitgeist in the **Green** movement. "Green theory" or the Green philosophy is a desire by consumers to "do good." The decisions we make are based on our set of values. Values are beliefs about the importance of something. For example, most businesses value an employee with a college education because they feel education will benefit their business. With regard to dress, values affect our choices in what to wear. Personal beliefs, such as how the environment should be treated, have an impact on fashion purchases. A growing portion of consumers are using their fashion purchases as advocacy for a better world by purchasing items that are sustainable or eco-friendly.

Beginning in the 1960s people started to become cognizant of their impact on the environment. Rivers and skies were polluted, forests were being decimated, and landfills were overcrowded with discarded clothes. By the 21st century the earth's population has surpassed 7 billion and people became more aware of their carbon footprint and the impact their actions held, including their clothing purchases. For example, to manufacture one t-shirt up to 700 gallons of water are used (Wallender,

Figure 4.2 This 1949 Dior ensemble, made in the New Look style, illustrates the return to femininity after WWII with a low neckline and voluminous skirt. The Ohio State University Historic Costume and Textiles Collection.

2012), not to mention the chemicals used for dyeing or the energy used for transportation, spinning, weaving, cutting and sewing. Resources such as water and plants had died or dried up on some continents and what was left was being polluted from factory run-offs, human-caused disasters such as oil spills, and overharvesting of oceans and lands. As people became more aware of the damage the fashion industry was doing to the environment they advocated for earth-friendly or "green" fashion. Whereas prior generations had neglected the environment, new generations began to understand and see the impact of decades of abuse.

Consumers of green products regularly seek information on garment tags and packaging relative to the materials used in the item (Phau and Ong, 2007) and such information-seeking has increased in recent years (Hyllegard, Yan, Ogle & Lee, 2012). Retailers and merchandisers have responded to the Green movement by shifting their manufacturing model to be more eco-conscious, designers have launched green lines, and companies advertise "giving back" a percentage of their profits to the community or organizations. Green fashion, sometimes referred to as eco chic, incorporates sustainable methods into the design, manufacture, and sale of goods. Sustainability usually opposes the concept of fashion, where an item is discarded not because it lost its physical utility but because it lost its popularity. However, sustainability has found a niche in the fashion industry. The new sustainable practices include limiting the use of chemical pesticides, dyes, and fabrics, recycling products, utilizing renewable resources, and manufacturing under fair conditions. For some, the Green movement also incorporates the "radius" zone philosophy, which is buying goods that are made within a pre-determined radius of one's home (e.g., 10 miles/kilometers). This not only reduces transportation costs and waste (e.g., gas) but also supports the local economy. The Green movement has also spurred individuals to recycle clothing and wear vintage garments. The consumer has more options when it comes to recycled clothing and also more ability to be unique. However, some consumers may not necessarily be interested in the environmental aspect of the movement but rather that it is now a social norm (Kim, Lee, & Hur, 2012). Hence, the concept of Green itself is fashionable.

Many of today's fashions and clothing choices reflect this philosophy. Locally-made products reduce oil and gas use compared to if they were made offshore and had to be shipped. Vintage and thrift stores, once thought of having out-of-date, poor-quality clothing, have gained a positive reputation by offering recycled clothing. Restyling one's wardrobe is encouraged and YouTube videos, advice columns, and blogs offer ways to update last season's fashions. This movement represents a shift in the way people think about themselves, the earth, and the way people impact the earth.

Businesses are responding to this consumer demand too. Textile growers are offering organic cotton—grown without the use of pesticides or fertilizers—and hemp is offered as a sustainable alternative because it can be grown without pesticides or fertilizers. Colorists are trying new methods of dyeing; historically, traditional method of dyeing resulted in waste water contaminated with left-over pigment. If the dye was synthetic this means that chemicals were discarded too. Usually they were discarded into rivers or burned and absorbed by the atmosphere. Some colorists are experimenting with natural dyes, but they tend not to be as color-fast as chemical dyes, meaning their color fades. A new technology created by Colorep called AirDye™ is offering a sustainable solution to wet dyeing. Rather than diluting dyes in water, the dye is injected directly onto the textile and absorbed by the fiber. Currently, the technology only works with synthetic fibers.

Spatial diffusion

The concept of **spatial diffusion** comes from the discipline of geography and posits that there are areas where fashion trends develop and are first seen (such as London, New York City, Paris, or Tokyo). Neighboring areas then see the style and adopt it and neighboring areas to those neighboring areas repeat the process. It acts like a pebble dropped into a calm river. The pebble represents the style and the first ring created represents the immediate surrounding area, with each successive ring representing an area adjacent to the previous ring, but further from the center origin. You could also think of it as a variation of the classic Trickle Down theory (see Chapter 3, p. 57) but rather than successive classes adopting the fashion, it is successive geographic areas that adopt the fashion. This has been observed in a number of past fashion trends, including grunge style which originated in Seattle, and Casual Friday which originated in Hawai'i.

Grunge. In the case of grunge, originating in the mid-1980s, Seattle, Washington was the epicenter for the trend. The grunge music scene was the inspiration for this fashion, for grunge musicians in Seattle had a unique style unto themselves that included flannel shirts and an overall thrift-store look that looked affordable (or cheap, depending on your perspective) and well-worn (or dirty, depending on your perspective). It looked overall "grungy." While it originated in Seattle it eventually spread to the states of Washington, California, and beyond. In 1993 three designers presented collections inspired by the grunge subculture: Anna Sui, Christian Francis Roth, and Marc Jacobs for Perry Ellis (see Figure 4.3). Jacobs was later released from his contract (or fired, depending on your perspective) with Perry Ellis because his designs did not sell. It was not that the designs were not good or that he was not spot-on with the trend, but high-end grunge was an oxymoron. Grunge was a do-it-yourself look acquired from thrift stores and was relatively inexpensive to achieve, so people were not going to pay high-end prices for a designer-created garment when the authentic look was easy to find and afford.

Casual Friday. Casual Friday dress was a mode of dressing in the United States in the 1980s and 1990s that meant that people working in office settings could "dress down" every Friday. It was thought to promote a positive work environment and productivity. Linda Arthur (2008) wrote that Casual Fridays had its origins in

Figure 4.3 Marc Jacobs' grunge collection for Perry Ellis drew inspiration from street style but was a commercial flop. George Chinsee/WWD © Condé Nast 1992.

Hawai'i, where Aloha Fridays were popular in the 1960s. On Aloha Fridays people were encouraged to wear casual Hawaiian-style clothing. Arthur argued that residents who lived in Hawai'i during this time eventually moved to California where they promoted the casual dressing routine in their offices. Eventually, the notion spread and office workers across the United States were swathed in jeans, khakis, t-shirts, and sneakers on any given Friday. The fashion for Casual Fridays eventually died down as work-dress codes became more relaxed in general and people started dressing casually Monday through Friday.

The theory of spatial diffusion was useful to explain fashion dissemination for most of the history of fashion and it also served to explain why urban centers were considered chic but the outskirts and rural areas were called provincial. However, since the advent of the Internet, fashions and styles that are shown in one city can be immediately telecast around the world, thus making the dissemination broader and its adoption more dependent on information technology rather than proximity.

Subcultural or style tribes/collective behavior

Sometimes groups of people are the inspiration for new fashions. Sociologist Herbert Blumer (1962) termed this **"collective selection,"** while anthropologist Ted Polhemus (1994) termed this "style tribes." **Style tribes** have unique looks that identify them in a particular category, such as punk, goth, lipstick lesbian, rock-a-billy, Lolita, and Teddy Boy. When a subculture is known for a particular aesthetic and that style is valued or appreciated by others, it is adopted into the mainstream. So while you can have a specific group of people who are authentic punk and live the life of a punk, the punk style can be worn by others who are not necessarily true punks but like the look.

Note how this concept relates to spatial diffusion. Many subcultures originate in a specific city where neighboring cities see them (e.g., Mods originated in London, Lolita in Tokyo, Hippies in San Francisco). As they adopt the style (due to geographic location) they are also disseminating the cultural look. In addition this phenomenon is representative of Ted Polhemus' concept of "street style" where fashions originate on the street. Three style tribes are presented that illustrate the adoption of a subcultural style into a broader fashion system: Guido, cowboy, and nerd.

Guido. The Guido style originated in New Jersey, United States, during the 1970s (Tricarico, 2008). It developed around young men of Italian descent who enjoyed dancing in discos and styled themselves in tight-fitting apparel that revealed the body's silhouette and greased-back hair styles. The Guido style incorporates a lifestyle of partying, body maintenance (including tanning, weight-training, removing body hair and shaping eyebrows), and appropriating clothing that reveals the body. This style originated in working-class areas of New Jersey but has been adopted by others who find the aesthetic appealing. Reality television featured the lifestyle in shows like "Growing Up Gotti" (which starred Victoria Gotti, the daughter of Gambino Mafia Don John Gotti, and her sons), "Jersey Shore" (see Figure 4.4), "Jersey Couture," and "Jerseylicious" disseminated the look and lifestyle to viewers. Some of the reality stars of "Jersey Shore" have launched their own fashion product lines including apparel and fragrance; Mike "The Situation" Sorrentino launched "The Sitch" cologne and fashion line "Situation Nation" and Jennifer "J-Woww" Farley launched Filthy Couture. Retail stores (such as Guido Fashions in Florida), blogs, videos and how-to guides on the Internet offer people tips about what brands to buy and how to achieve the perfect Guido look.

The appeal of the style was likely due the fact that it mirrored the Zeitgeist. The in-your-face sexuality, the body-conscious, designer-labeled clothing, and the tanning regime were reflections of the early 2000s liberal attitudes towards casual sex (or "hooking-up"), status ideals, partying, glorification of the toned body, and technological advancements in tanning salons and tanning creams.

Cowboys. Cowboys are an easily-recognized group given their iconic Stetson hats, blue denim jeans, bandanas, leather chaps, and boots. Their attire developed out of necessity when cowboys were working in sunny climates amid rough conditions in Spain, Mexico, and the United States (Wilson, 2008). Real cowboys such as Theodore Roosevelt, rodeo performers such as "Buffalo Bill" Cody and Tom

Figure 4.4   The cast of the American television series "Jersey Shore" helped to disseminate the Guido aesthetic. Helga Esteb/Shutterstock.com.

Mix, and fictional characters such as the Lone Ranger, the Marlboro Man, and J. R. Ewing helped disseminate the look to the broader public. It became fashionable to dress like a cowboy and fashion designers have responded appropriately over time. Ralph Lauren has regularly adopted the cowboy look for his collections, while D&G offered cowgirl options for early 2010.

Australian cowboys, called ringers, have also instigated fashion trends. In the Outback the same need for protective apparel applied as it did to the United States' West. Oil-cloth[1] coats kept ringers dry and warm while the distinctive Akubura hat kept the sun off of their face. The Akubra hat (see Figure 4.5), made of the undercoat of rabbit pelts, eventually became a symbol of Australian masculinity. In the 1970s it was adopted as a national symbol of Australia. The style was picked up by designers and a trend in retail stores in Australia and the United States in the 1990s and 2000s (Saethre, 2012).

The cowboy style—or at least elements of it—has become a classic staple of the wardrobe, though it does have periods where it is more popular. The enduring look is likely due to the romanticized myth of the cowboy as a rugged, heroic survivalist.

Nerd Chic. Intellectuals have long been viewed as the antithesis to anything chic or stylish so it is with some surprise that their look had become fashionable in the early 2010s (see Figure 4.6) Granted, some typical elements of the prototypical nerd look—blemished skin, greasy hair—were not adopted, but other elements were. Nerd chic, or geek chic as it is sometimes called, included glasses (even fake ones for those who have perfect eyesight), a shirt buttoned all the way to the collar, sweater-vest or blue blazer, suspenders, high-water pants[2], and an accessory such as a bowtie, computer bag, or large vintage-style head phones around the neck. Fashion leaders such as Justin Timberlake, Scarlett Johansson, and Tyra Banks have all appropriated an "adorkable" look at one time or another. However, nerd chic does not mean copying the nerd aesthetic point for point; rather, the looks are toned down and only specific elements are fashionable.

Nerd chic likely became fashionable for a few reasons.

1. There was a social shift in affluence. The rise of Silicon Valley as the center of the computer industry led to the rise of entrepreneurs and managers with desirable computer skills. The jock with a hot body of yesteryear was replaced by the nerd with a hot mind.
2. Films about the nerd-hero became blockbusters. *Juno, Napoleon Dynamite*, and *The 40-year Old Virgin* were a radical shift from the *Revenge of the Nerds* films; no longer were intellectuals portrayed as socially-incompetent but were now snarky and sassy.
3. Thin is in. Whereas the curvaceous woman or muscular man was once the ideal, a thin body aesthetic had replaced it, and nerds, who cultivated their mind over their body, met this ideal. As discussed in Chapter 2, the slender silhouette, spearheaded by Hedi Slimane, became popular.
4. Irony was important. One of the tenets of postmodernism is irony (Morgado, 1996), or a wry sense of juxtaposition or contradiction. And what is more ironic than taking something completely undesirable and making it fashionable?

Figure 4.5 The fashionable Australian Akubura hat and oil-cloth jacket were inspired by real-life ringers who needed them for practical purposes. They eventually became fashionable components and worn by men from different walks of life. Christopher Meder – Photography/Shutterstock.com.

Figure 4.6 This comic by Jen Sorensen illustrates the irony of the Nerd or Geek Chic style. Jen Sorensen.

Cultural authentication

Cultural acculturation (Eicher & Erikosima, 1980) occurs when two cultures come into contact and one culture incorporates aspects or artifacts from the other culture into its own culture. "The construct of cultural authentication applies to specific articles and ensembles of dress identified as ethnic and considered indigenous when the users are not the makers or when the material used is not indigenous in origin" (Eicher & Erikosima, 1995, p. 140). Eicher and Erikosima (1980) proposed four phases to cultural authentication: selection, characterization, incorporation, and transformation. *Selection* occurs when an artifact is identified and adopted by the new culture. *Characterization* occurs when meaning is given to the new artifact. *Incorporation* occurs when the new artifact is given a functional role. And, *transformation* occurs when the artifact is altered from its original form to make it distinct to the new culture. Though Eicher and Erokosima proposed this order, dress historian Linda Arthur (1997) observed that the order can be changed.

Eicher and Erokosima's (1980) concept of cultural authentication was developed after observing the Kalabari people's use of textile products unique to their culture. The Kalabari people live in the delta of the southern part of Nigeria and wear a wrapper made of distinctive cloth imported from India and transformed into a Kalabari textile. The cloth is made from imported lightweight, colorful cotton fabrics of which threads are cut and removed. They call the fabric pelete-bit (cut thread) or fimate-bit (pulled thread) depending on the method used to extract threads. While the materials used to create the wrappers are imported, the designs are traditional to the Kalabari. Selection occurred when cotton fabric was chosen "for self-enhancement and for making a statement about positive self-acceptance" (p. 50). Eicher and Erokosima argued the result is that "the 'dressed-up' person is valued at a level different from that of the same person attired for work and production" (p. 50). Thus, the Indian fabric is *selected* by a group. The cloth is then characterized (or named)—the Kalabari named it pelete-bit or fimate-bit—thus giving the cloth and wearer status. Incorporation occurred when the cloth was worn for special occasions to show lineage. And transformation occurred when the cloth was worn to show membership in the Kalabari culture.

Eicher (2004) later revisited the topic of cultural authentication among the Kalabari and observed what she called a ping-pong effect. The Indian suppliers of the cloth that the Kalabari used began to make manufactured versions of the pelete-bit. This new version of the pelete-bit was sold to the Kalabari but was also adapted by an Indian designer who created the design on silk scarves for a global market. Thus, the fabric originated in India, transformed in Nigeria as a new product, was transformed again in India as a new product.

Arthur (1997) used cultural authentication to explain the adoption of European/American style of clothing into Hawaiian culture but noted that the order was different from that offered by Erokosima and Eicher (1981). In Arthur's research, characterization was the last step of the process. Hawaiian women traditionally wore a wrapper-type garment, made of kapa cloth (pounded mulberry bark), called a pa'u. When the missionaries began arriving in Hawai'i in 1820, Hawaiian women began to adopt their style of dress and created a garment known as the holokū. Arthur's analysis shows cultural authentication went from selection, transformation, incorporation, and characterization.

Selection: With the arrival of foreigners, royal Hawaiians (ali'i) adopted European and American fabrics, which were softer and more durable than kapa. Hawaiian royal women also admired the dress styles of missionary women, which were typically high-waisted with narrow sleeves and a narrow skirt, and sought to have similar dresses made for them.

Transformation: Dowager queen Kalakua requested a dress in the new style. Missionary women, who could sew the garment, adapted the European style for the

---

91

warm climate and made the form looser to fit the queen's ample girth. They replaced the high waist with a yoke. "The end result was a basic design which was simply a full, straight skirt attached to a yoke with a high neck and tight sleeves" (Arthur, 1997, p. 132). The style was adopted by other ali'i women but was never worn by missionary wives. Hawaiian women wore the holokū with traditional Hawaiian accessories such as the lei and pa'u. Some Hawaiian commoners copied the holokū design but used kapa as their fabric. By the 1870s a train was added to the holokū.

Incorporation: The holokū was originally worn by the ali'i women for special occasions. It was considered an upper-class garment. But as western notions of modesty and clothing the body were incorporated into Hawaiian culture, the holokū trickled down to the commoner women as an acceptable and desirable form of dress.

Characterization: It is difficult to say when the dress was named the holokū because Hawaiian language was not written. The term likely came into use 1845–1865, but was definitely in print by 1865. Since then it has been "exclusively associated with Hawaiian women" (Arthur, 1997, p. 137) (see Figure 4.7).

Fashion as modernity

When something is modern it means it reflects contemporary sentiments, ideas, and technology and is usually in contrast to (or displaces) older sentiments, ideas, or technology. Fashion is often considered modern, because fashion at its very core is the representation of new aesthetics or new ideas. The development of the European system of fashion is linked to Europe's change from a feudal structure to an industrial and capitalist system (Wilson, 1987). This change represented new beliefs and a break from the past. As such, the development of fashion—and those who had fashionable clothing—represented the new era and way of thinking. "The growth of fashion, or changing styles of dress, is associated with what has been termed 'the civilizing process' in Europe" (p. 13). Fashion became a designation of the modern lifestyle. Those with fashion were considered modern, whereas those without fashion were designated as primitive.

In this section, two examples are offered that illustrate the influence of **modernity** or desire to appear modern. The first is Japan's embrace of western fashion aesthetics and dress forms as the country emerged from two centuries of little to no contact with other nations. The second is of Coco Chanel and how her aesthetic represented the modern woman by incorporating modernist principles into her designs.

Japan

In Europe and North America, dress had centuries to transform from pre-modern to modern styles. Both geographic regions saw people transform from an agrarian or feudal society to one that was built on commerce and rational thought. This period

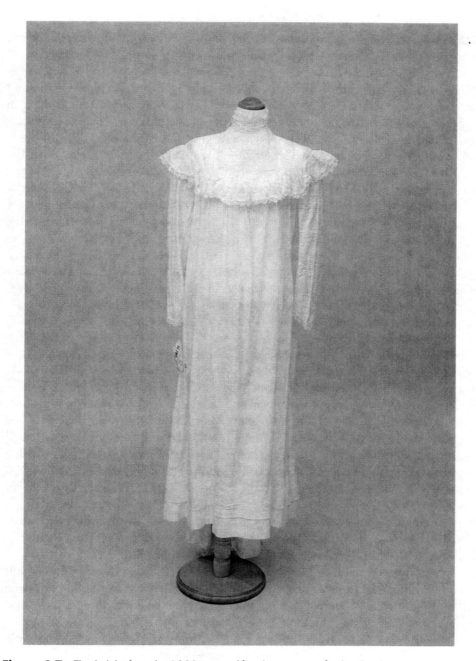

Figure 4.7 This holokū from the 1900s exemplifies the concept of cultural authentication; western concepts of sewing and modesty were incorporated into Hawaiian modes of dress. University of Hawai'i Historic Costume Collection.

of time was called the Enlightenment and the events of the Enlightenment transformed society by replacing superstition and assumption with science and experience.

Meanwhile, Japan was in a self-imposed exile or *sakoku*. In the 1600s Japan severed contact with other countries in an effort to stop outside influences and build a prosperous nation. Only Holland and China were permitted to trade in Nagasaki. Contact with foreigners could result in execution for Japanese nationals. Japan remained in isolation until 1854 when American Naval Commodore Matthew Calbraith Perry forced Japan to begin trading with the United States by signing the Treaty of Kanagawa. Japan was suddenly thrust into the modern world and now had to compete with advanced technology, innovations, and challenging philosophies.

In an effort to become "modern" Japan had to change its style of dressing. Prior to the opening of Japan, Japanese citizens wore loose-fitting garments (today, generally known as kimono) that were wrapped around the body. This was a one-size-fits-all garment where the fabric could be folded and tucked as a person aged or their body shape changed. Traditional Japanese dress was perceived by the West as lacking fashion trends; although certain colors and motifs were appropriate for certain seasons and garments were worn year after year. Japanese clothing was imbued with custom and tradition which was contrary to the western fashion system that embraced frequent change.

European and North American clothing was quite different from the loose Japanese garments. European and North American clothing was fitted to the body and styles changed based on concepts of fashionableness. In an effort to appear modern, Japanese workers started to wear western clothing for business but Japanese clothing otherwise (Slade, 2009). It was important for Japanese people to be viewed as equals to the outside world; traditional clothing made them look quaint and foreign, but western clothing made them appear contemporary. Eventually wearing western-style clothing beyond the office was adopted and helped build an image of modernity for its people (Slade, 2009). The concept of fashion from the West for Japan was about demonstrating equality and modernity on a large scale. "Fashion was a modern desire for newness in Japan, not a means of class differentiation, because Japanese nation identity was, and is, configured different from identity in the West, where class was, and perhaps still is, more central" (p. 52).

What is different about this explanation of fashion change from others is that typically fashion change is an evolution, but for Japan it was abrupt. The European and North American system of fashion had developed as a way to depict class (as explained by the Trickle Down theory, see Chapter 3, p. 57) but in Japan the sudden shift was not about class, but about shedding old for new. The change was not slow and fluid, as in Europe and North America, but was sudden.

Coco Chanel

We can also see the influence of modernity when we examine the work of Gabrielle "Coco" Chanel. As a fashion designer, Coco Chanel was a visionary who sought to unburden women from the wardrobe regime of corsets, long skirts, and constricting silhouettes. Chanel viewed these modes of dress as old-fashioned and sought to emancipate women with new concepts. Chanel appropriated fabrics that were hereto used exclusively for menswear: jersey knit, flannel, corduroy, and tweed (Driscoll, 2010; Wilson, 2003). She appropriated staple items from men's wardrobes as well: cardigan sweaters, trousers, and trench coats. She also combined traditional dressmaking techniques of draping with traditional menswear tailoring (Koda, 2005). In doing so she challenged expected notions of gender roles and embraced modern thinking of equality. The women's movement of the early 20th century focused on gender parity. Advocates demanded the right to vote, equal pay, and equal rights. The clothes Chanel designed and borrowed from men were more comfortable and provided more ease of movement, compared to what women had been wearing. The aesthetic she created was a very modern one; Chanel's approach to streamlined, practical clothing signaled the modernist aesthetic of effortlessness (Steele, 1998). Prior generations had a fashion aesthetic that looked like effort was put into the selection and care of clothing. Chanel's style (whether or not effort was actually made) at least looked like none was made.

Two features of the modernist movement of the early 20th century were industrialization and capitalism. Chanel's designs reflected both of these. She embraced ready-to-wear manufacturing and replicated her designs on a large scale. Her designs, therefore, were worn by more women than say a couturier who produced only one design at a time. Simultaneously, she was also a capitalist who commanded a growing business. One of her innovations was costume jewelry. Driscoll (2010) also argues that Chanel's use of costume jewelry underscores aesthetics rather than wealth. Whereas prior, only genuine jewels and gems were appropriate adornment, the bits of colored glass chains and faux pearls that Chanel designed and sold allowed women of all classes to wear decorative accessories. The use of costume jewelry was part of the total look of the modern "Chanel" woman.

Chanel's industry and capitalism also extended to her fragrance enterprise. Her signature fragrance, Chanel No. 5, was also a departure from existing fragrances, and also embraced the modernist concept of the abstract. Abstract means to exist as an idea but not in reality. Chanel No. 5 was an abstract fragrance. Prior to Chanel No. 5 fragrances were typically one note, meaning they were comprised of one scent. Additionally, they were also called by that note. A perfume called "Rose" smelled like a rose, "Jasmine" smelled like jasmine, "Lily of the Valley" smelled like lily-of-the-valley, and so forth. Chanel's concoction, developed by perfumier Ernest Beaux, was a mixture of floral notes (or scents). It was a floral abstract, meaning it smelled like flowers, but not one specific flower. Among the floral notes included were rose, jasmine, iris, and lily-of-the-valley. The design of the flaçon for Chanel No. 5 also embraced modernist sensibilities. The silhouette was streamlined and simple, compared to prior flaçons that were ornate and decorative. The label was stark black and white and CHANEL was boldly printed larger than the perfume's name. This represented a new—or modern—approach to marketing, where the brand was more important than the item.

BOXED CASE 4.1: YAKUZA AS SUBCULTURAL STYLE AND SPATIAL DIFFUSION

The Yakuza are outlaw gang members of Japan who are involved in organized crime. The Mafia would be an Italian equivalent and the Bratva would be the Russian equivalent. The Yakuza has its roots in the early years of the Tokugawa Shogunate (1600–1868) when society was divided into a rigid class structure. People who could not cope with the rigid class structure or were not part of a legitimate class found acceptance in the Yakuza. In Japan, refined, simple attire was *de rigueur* for social interactions, but the Yakuza eschewed social protocol and flaunted their lifestyle with vibrant clothing and colorful skin. The Yakuza are recognizable by the tattoos which cover most of their body, called irezumi.

In Japan's history tattoos were sometimes fashionable and sometimes used for punishment. Someone who committed an illegal act was branded with a tattoo on his or her arms or head to designate their status as a criminal; such people were ostracized from society. In order to hide the brands people began to conceal them with decorative, colorful, flourishing tattoos. Tattoos were outlawed in Japan when the nation began trading with foreigners after 200 years of imposed seclusion, because tattoos did not align with the image of a sophisticated, modern culture. During this time they were also associated with criminal behavior. Tattooing remained illegal in Japan until 1948, though perceptions about the link between criminal behavior and tattoos remain constant. Today in Japan, people with visible tattoos are not permitted in some restaurants or public baths.

To join a Yakuza clan a potential member person would have their skin tattooed with the clan's crest. This not only showed allegiance, but the process of getting the painful tattoo also demonstrated strength and endurance. People with tattoos were not allowed in many areas of society, so by default when a man decorated his body with irezumi not only was he entering one world (the Yakuza) but leaving another as well (mainstream society).

Meanwhile, Japanese tattoo artists were hired to visit Europe and America to share their art and knowledge, while visitors to Japan acquired tattoos and others tried to replicate them. One westerner who helped bring the art of irezumi to the West was "Sailor Jerry" Collins. Collins was a sailor in the United States Navy and visited Japan where he learned the art of Japanese tattooing from a master. He settled in Honolulu, Hawai'i and opened a tattoo parlor in 1960 and is among the first tattoo artists to have Japanese-style tattoos in his portfolio. His work on visitors to the Hawaiian Islands helped disseminate the style worldwide. (Poysden & Bratt, 2006).

Today irezumi-style "sleeves" and "suits" are popular (see Figure 4.8) but for those who do not want ink under their skin other options are available. Ed Hardy's elaborate designs also evoke the irezumi tattoo (incidentally, he was a student of Sailor Jerry) and sheer shirts and leggings with irezumi designs printed on them were popular by the late 2000s and gave the wearer the look of full-body tattoo without the permanence, pain, or price.

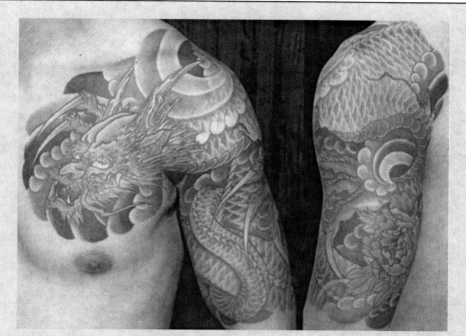

Figure 4.8 Yakuza-style irezumi sleeves demonstrate a fashion trend inspired by subcultural style and spatial diffusion. Billy Whitney, 808 Tattoo.

BOXED CASE 4.2: ETHICS FOCUS: AKIHIKO IZUKURA

Akihiko Izukura is a renowned textile artist and clothing designer from Kyoto, Japan who embraces a no-waste philosophy when it comes to designing and producing apparel. He works mostly with silk and uses natural dyes that come from nature, such as walnut, madder, clove, and cochineal insects. When he dyes fibers he uses the entire liquid dye; nothing is wasted. During the dyeing process, with each successive dyeing the dye strength is weaker and the resulting color is lighter. Izukura explains this becomes part of the design: "You have to plan your design ahead. You have to know what [portion of the garment] will be light and dark" (personal communication, February 2011). This meticulous attention to detail may be challenging, but it underscores his philosophy.

His design philosophy is based on ancient Japanese teachings where one respects nature and the environment. In his silk weaving he uses the entire silk cocoon, the long filament fiber, as well as the noil, or the shorter fibers that are usually discarded. This gives texture to the resulting fabric. Izukura explains: "Natural dyeing comes from *life* of animals and plants. Man should make the most of deriving it, not just deliberately select what suits their tastes. The concept of superiority between nature and man is meaningless. 'A thoughtful sense of beauty' comes only from the respect of what is truly a beauty. It is not a 'discerning sense of beauty.' " (http://www.akihikoizukura.com/)

Summary

Fashion at the cultural level is a lens through which one can examine values and beliefs of a group of people. These values are often seen through the Zeitgeist and the subsequent people, events, technology, ideals, and attitudes that dominate a time period. These elements can be expressed in subcultures that influence trends among larger groups of people or are "exchanged" when two cultures with unique features come into contact with each other in what can be considered a paradigm shift. In addition, because cultures are frequently geographically-based, fashion can spread from region to region. Thus, fashion at the cultural level has the potential to change daily life activities.

Key Terms

- Characterization
- Collective selection
- Cultural authentication
- Green
- Incorporation
- Modernity

- Selection
- Spatial diffusion
- Style tribes
- Transformation
- Zeitgeist

Discussion questions

1. Discuss cultural cliques in your high school and how their clothing reflected their culture.
2. One of the complaints about locally-manufactured goods is that they cost more to produce and therefore cost more at the retail level. How can you persuade consumers to embrace and to partake in the Green movement and purchase locally-made garments?

Learning activities

1. Use Nystrom's framework to identify the Zeitgeist for a particular decade. Relate the Zeitgeist to the fashions of the era.
2. Examine the attire of female or male country-western singers to note changes in clothing. How have the garments changed over the years and how does it reflect cultural changes in country-western music and culture? Examples to examine: Dolly Parton, Faith Hill, Shania Twain, Tammy Wynette, the Mandrel Sisters, Reba MacIntire, Billy Ray Cyrus, Willie Nelson, Hank Williams, Johnny Cash, Garth Brooks, and Brad Paisley.
3. Examine commercials—how many fashions were based on culture? Which cultures were used as inspiration?

Notes

1. A fabric which has been boiled or coated with oil to make it waterproof.
2. Pants that are short and reveal the ankle, looking as if the wearer has outgrown them.

Further reading

Balascescu, A., (2003). Tehran chic: Islamic headscarves, fashion designers, and the new geographies of modernity. *Fashion Theory, 7* (1), 39–56.

Hansen, K. T. (2004). The world in dress: Anthropological perspectives on clothing, fashion, and culture. *Annual Review of Anthropology, 33,* 369–392.

Kawakami, B. F. (1993). *Japanese Immigrant Clothing in Hawaii 1885–1941.* Honolulu, Hawai'i: University of Hawai'i Press.

Ugolini, L. (2009). Clothing and the modern man in 1930s Oxford. In P. McNeil and V. Karaminas [eds] *The Men's Fashion Reader* (pp. 299–309). Oxford: Berg.

Welters, L. (2005). The Beat generation: Subcultural style. In L. Welters and P. A. Cunningham [eds] *Twentieth-century American Fashion* (pp. 145–168). Oxford: Berg.

Vinken, B. (2005). *Fashion Zeitgeist: Trends and Cycles in the Fashion System.* Oxford: Berg.

5

THE FASHION SYSTEM[1]

The western fashion system is a complex assortment of industries that work together and in tandem to produce, promote, and sell new products. Within the fashion system are forecasters, designers, manufacturers, marketers, merchandisers, sales representatives, managers, promoters, and retailers, each of whom has a role in fostering fashion change. What they decide to produce (or not produce), promote (or not promote) ultimately affects what may become fashion. It is necessary to understand that while businesses have a role in developing new styles, consumers have an equally important role in accepting new styles. Ultimately, consumers have to adopt the new style en masse for it to become a fashion.

The fashion industry is segmented into levels based on price point and relative quality. At the top of the list is haute couture. ***Haute couture*** is high-end, one-of-a-kind garments that are produced for a limited clientele. In haute couture the client will visit the designer who will take measurements or even construct a dress form to the exact measurements of the client's body. The design will be handmade from the finest fabrics and once completed the pattern and muslins will be destroyed. True haute couture houses are members of **La Chambre Syndicale de la Couture**, a governing body for the industry. The cost of one garment can be in the thousands of Euros or United States dollars. One estimate is that there are approximately 2,000 haute couture clients in the world (Craik, 2009), but despite the small number of haute couture customers, it is a vital component of the industry because of the press it receives. Haute couture fashion shows are industry events that have become popular forms of entertainment. Celebrities with no or little connection to the fashion industry vie for seats to the shows. The shows are reported in popular consumer newspapers and magazines, as well as in industry periodicals such as *Women's Wear Daily*. The shows are found online, posted in Facebook, tweeted on Twitter, and passed around on Instagram. A lot of buzz is generated from a small number of garments.

Designer categories follow haute couture and include well-known brands, such as Gucci, Prada, Marc Jacobs, and Dior. They use quality fabrics and are generally at the forefront of fashion. Many designer categories lead the industry in innovative designs or innovative use of new materials. Pieces can sell for US$1,000 or more. The designer category is followed by **Bridge** (price points generally under US$1,000), **Better** (price points under US$500), **Moderate** (price points under $100), and **budget** (price points under $50). These categories are generally made in factories, and as the price point descends, so too do the quality of fabrics and craftsmanship.

One of the most important components of producing and selling new products is making sure the intended audience is aware of the product, and more importantly, making sure the intended audience likes and wants your product. In marketing, there is a concept that posits that the more a person is exposed to something, the more familiar it becomes, and consequently the more it is liked. This is called the *mere exposure hypothesis*. In fashion, we can adopt this hypothesis to argue that the more a fashion style is seen by the public the more it will be liked (and subsequently purchased and worn). The fashion system uses this concept to promote new styles by showing them repeatedly in commercials, in magazine advertisements, product placements (such as at red carpet events), and visual display. The hope is that even if someone did not like the style upon initial viewing, by seeing it on television, in magazines, on celebrities, and in store displays, the viewer will eventually come to appreciate and purchase it. This is an overarching construct that you should remember as you read this chapter because the business of fashion is the business of repetition.

In this chapter you will read about theories and concepts that explain who controls the production of new styles; how new styles reach different markets; the role technology plays in fashion; how designers, merchandisers, and product developers get inspiration from the past; and how merchandisers create unique brand identities to differentiate their merchandise mix from competitors' products.

Market Infrastructure theory

As a designer, you may develop the most wonderful, most beautiful dress that anyone has ever seen. It is the perfect color, the right fabric, and looks great on all body types; but if a merchandiser does not manufacture it, or a buyer does not buy it, or a retailer does not promote and sell it, it will not become a fashion because not enough people will be exposed to it, know about it, and want to wear it. It will not reach what Gladwell (2002) called the tipping point (see Chapter 1, p. 18).

Market Infrastructure theory argues that only clothing sold in retail environments can become fashion. While a trend may start in an innocuous area, it takes the entire fashion complex to make the trend into a fashion. The reason is because the merchandisers and retailers make the style available to everyone. When the Mod look began in London, if retailers around the globe did not carry the style it would have never been available for other demographics to buy. They may have seen it on television or in magazines, but without the availability of retail stores the trend would have never become as large as it did.

The gatekeepers of fashion are the ones responsible for scouting and bringing new fashions to the masses. A **gatekeeper** is someone who holds power. At a dam, the gatekeeper is responsible for regulating the flow of water into a valley; when the water builds up behind the dam, the gatekeeper is responsible for releasing water into the river. Designers, merchandisers, buyers, and retailers are all gatekeepers of fashion. Their job is to control the flow and ebb of fashions. Designers are responsible for predicting trends and their job is to translate the trends into wearable garments. Sometimes they work independently and sell their designs to retail buyers and sometimes they may work for a company under the direction of a merchandiser. Merchandisers are responsible for researching a market, scouting sources for fabrics, trims, buttons, and manufacturers, and setting sales goals. Buyers are responsible for selecting garments that designers create to sell in a retail environment. Buyers have to know their customers' demographics and psychographics in order to predict what their customers will want. Retailers are responsible for providing a space for the designs and promoting them through advertising and visual display. Each segment—designer, merchandiser, buyer, and retailer—has a role in selecting which styles are offered en masse to the public. They hold power as gatekeepers by analyzing trends and determining which trends they want to flow into the market. They also have the power to determine what should not be sold anymore. Based on the concept of planned obsolescence (as discussed in Chapter 1), that fashions are created to exist for only a short period of time, once a gatekeeper observes that the style has reached its maximum popularity, the gatekeepers discard it and bring in the next trend.

Gatekeepers must be keen to understand other aspects of fashion—the psychology, sociology, and culture of people—in order to design, select, and promote the trends. Simply featuring a garment in a store does not mean the style will become fashion. It must appeal to the customer on an aesthetic, psychological, sociological, and/or cultural level. You may be a fur designer and design the most luxurious lynx coat, it may have been bought and promoted through a retail store, but if the social climate of the area where the store is located is anti-fur, in all likelihood your design will not sell and will not become a fashion.

Trickle Across theory

Trickle Across theory, also known as "mass market" or "simultaneous adoption," posits that fashion trends reach all markets at the same time. Thus the dispersal of a trend is not according to class, as predicted by the trickle up and trickle down theories. Rather, the fashion system coordinates the release of the trend through various channels. This is made possible by mass communication, mass production, and the growing middle class (Brannon, 2005). Although Behling (1985/1986) argued that designs do not reach all market simultaneously but take at least a year, it is important to remember that she was writing in a time when the marketing and technology was not as sophisticated as today. For example, since then, fast fashion (see Chapter 1 for an explanation) has expanded the quickness that a trend can reach multiple markets.

How is it possible that a trend can start in multiple places at once? There are three parts to this answer. First, fashion forecasting. Some designers or merchandisers have in-house fashion forecasters and some utilize independent services outside their company. Fashion forecasters predict upcoming and future trends by conducting research; they observe known fashion innovators and leaders, look at trends in street fashion, follow past trends to predict a return (see "Historic Continuity theory", Chapter 2, p. 45) and get a general idea for attitudes and responses to colors, fabrications, trims, and silhouettes. They then produce books and clients use these books when designing their upcoming lines or buying their stock. All levels of designers—from couture to budget—utilize some aspect of forecasting.

Second, many brands have different lines that reach different markets or price points. Ralph Lauren owns Polo, Chaps, Ralph Lauren Purple Label, Ralph Lauren Black Label, Ralph Lauren Sport, RLX, RRL, and Lauren. The Gap Company owns Banana Republic, Gap, Old Navy, Piperlime and Athleta. And the Burberry brands include Burberry Prorsum, Burberry London, Burberry Brit, Burberry Sport, Burberry Black, and Burberry Blue. Their goal is to reach as many different people via different markets as possible. When they forecast a new trend, they incorporate it into their different brands and lines by adjusting it for the particular customer. If bows are the trend, they might change the size, fabrication, or number used to reach the price point and consumer desire.

Third, **knock-offs** (or copies) can be produced quickly. Knock-offs began after World War II when discount manufacturers copied couture designs. While then there may have been a lag of weeks or months from copy to production, today a fashion can be knocked-off in days. Once a prominent fashion designer reveals a new line, scouts and competitors can digitally record the image, send it to their factories, and reproduce it at a different price point in a few days. This helps the trend reach more markets. More on knock-offs is discussed in the Ethics focus in this chapter.

Innovation theory

According to **Innovation theory** technology has long provided the fashion industry with new trends and provides the foundation for many fashions. Technology is the creation of new products and new ways of creating new products. Technology provides the fashion industry with (1) quicker production, (2) affordability, (3) new products, and (4) increased availability. In this section we will examine some technological innovations and how they spawned or created fashions.

Faster production. The cotton gin was created in 1793 by inventor Eli Whitney. Prior to its invention, cotton was hand-picked. Hand-picked cotton had to be cleaned by hand to remove dirt, debris, and seeds. The cotton gin helped to reduce the amount of time it took to clean cotton. Cotton was placed in a box that had combs and when a handle was wound, the gears rotated, cleaning the cotton. Two centuries later, the jacquard loom was created in 1908 by Joseph M. Jacquard. This invention streamlined the production of fabrics made with motifs incorporated into the actual weaving structure of the fabric. This resulted in a change in the aesthetics style of fabrics available.

Affordability. Technology can also make products affordable. Genuine jewels and gem stones are expensive due to their natural or manufactured limited availability. When a desired product is in short supply, the price is typically high. Such is the case with diamonds, sapphires, rubies, emeralds, and pearls. This situation provided engineers with an opportunity to create imitation products.

Whereas genuine diamonds are expensive, scientists sought ways to provide similar options. Cubic zirconia was released on the market in 1976 as one alternative to diamonds. Cubic zirconia occurs naturally, though it is very rare, but can also be created by humans. Compared to diamonds, its similar appearance with flawless character and affordability made it a desirable substitute and major trend by the early 1980s. It can be made in any color, but pink cubic zirconia was especially popular in the 1980s as well. Scientists have since used new technology to improve the quality of cubic zirconia to make it harder and shinier. Today, other diamond substitutes like synthetic moissanite offer alternatives to diamonds while flawless lab-created emeralds, sapphires, and rubies are also available as substitutes to their natural counterparts. This technology provides people with the opportunity to have gemstones at an affordable price.

Increased availability. Mikimoto Kokichi revolutionized the pearl industry with his innovative methods to create perfectly spherical pearls. Perfectly spherical pearls are rare to find in nature as most natural pearls are uniquely or oddly shaped. In nature, a pearl grows when a foreign object—such as a grain of sand—finds its way into an oyster. This irritates the oyster which produces shiny nacre to cover it. The longer the irritant remains, the more nacre is added, and the larger the pearl. In 1916 Mikimoto and his partner Tokishi Nishiawa patented a method whereby an irritant is purposefully planted into the oyster to create a pearl. This means that pearls could be created at will and availability increased. By the 1920s cultured pearls had become fashionable in Japan, and when the Japanese market was flooded with pearls Mikimoto launched a marketing campaign at world fairs and exhibitions in the United States and Europe, expanding his global reach. Today, strands of pearls are classic items in a woman's wardrobe (see Figure 5.1).

New products. Artificial fibers revolutionized the fashion industry. They were manufactured to mimic some of the properties of natural fibers (cotton, wool, silk, and flax) but improve on some of their weaker traits. For example, silk is soft and luxurious but wrinkles easily.

The first manufactured fiber was rayon and it was marketed as a substitute for expensive silk, due to similar soft handling and high sheen. It was made from naturally-occurring cellulose that was engineered into fibers. Early developments of

Figure 5.1 The availability of cultured pearls, made possible by Mikimoto, helped to make them a classic wardrobe staple. Jewelry courtesy of Marcia Morgado; image by Attila Pohlmann.

rayon date to the mid-1850s but it was not until the early 1900s that rayon was made commercially, and the 1940s that it became common. Nylon was the first truly synthetic fiber, made entirely of chemicals. Engineered by Dupont in 1935, by 1940 nylon stockings had become a viable substitute for silk stockings when silk was in short supply during World War II.

Other artificial fibers have since been produced and marketed, with some becoming fashion statements. Spandex found favor with consumers due to its elasticity as foundation garments and today is used in high-compression fabrics. Polyester gained favor in the 1960s and 1970s for its wrinkle-resistance and comfort. And faux fur, made from a variety of artificial fibers, is used as an alternative to real fur.

The invention of spray-on-fabrics such as Fabrican provides the latest technological advancement in textiles. Using an aerosol can, fibers and polymers are sprayed directly onto a person and quickly dry. The fibers bond together (but not to the body), can be removed from the person as a complete article of dress, and can be washed. Currently available, it has yet to influence fashion greatly due to its high price, but given its versatility, ease of use, and uniqueness we will likely see spray-on-fabrics as fashion in the future.

While these examples demonstrate how technology has influenced fashion, historian Vesna Matković (2010) has argued that at times fashion has influenced technology. She cites the development of knitting machines to keep up with the fashions of the times. Beginning in Elizabethan England, William Lee produced a knitting machine in 1589 to meet the demand for fine-knit stockings. Stockings made by hand took time and manufacturing could not keep up with demand, but the innovation of a new machine using steel knitting needles facilitated faster production. Matković further recognized that new machines or alterations to existing machines were made to increase availability of open-work gloves (1793), lace knitwear (1769), ribbed knits (1758), single jacquard patterns (1769), vertical stripes (1776), and jacquard patterns in multiple colors (1921). Matković argued that fashion influenced knitting technology until the development of computer assisted design (CAD) technology:

> It is difficult to say whether. . .fashion changes influenced the development of CAD/CAM technology or whether the development of a new generation of machines based on computer designing and computer production enabled them. This is a time when flat knitting machines could cover their greatest possibilities, i.e., they could knit everything that fashion required. (p. 137)

Historic resurrection

Bruce Oldfield, British fashion designer, has said fashion is "a gentle progression of revisited ideas." Fashion designers often look to the past and use **historic resurrection** for inspiration when creating new garments. In Chapter 4 when reading about the Zeitgeist you learned about Dior and how he turned to the Belle Epoch to get inspiration for his collection that became known as the New Look. Though designers look to the past, they must reinterpret past aesthetics for the current era (see Figures 5.2 and 5.3). The fashions of the 1980s were a reinterpretation of the 1940s.

Figure 5.2 Fashion designers often look to past styles when designing new products. The style of these 1890s men's shoes was revisited by Varvatos in the late 2000s (see Figure 5.3). Victoria and Albert Museum, London.

Figure 5.3 Varvatos shoes from the late 2000s. The style is based on shoes from the 1890s (see Figure 5.2). Shoes courtesy of author; image by Attila Pohlmann.

In the 1980s women in the United States were entering the workforce in droves and sought garments that embodied power and respectability while still maintaining femininity. The last time that women in the United States had entered the workforce in such numbers was in the 1940s during World War II. In the 1940s, due to fabric restrictions, women's garments were tailored. Suits with shoulder pads and tubular silhouettes with little frill and excess were common. These styles were reinterpreted for the 1980s: shoulder pads conveyed masculine authority, but peplums, vibrant colors, and supple fabrics such as rayon and silk conveyed femininity. In the late 2000s and early 2010s aspects of the 1980s returned. Torn, tight, acid-washed jeans were iconic during the 1980s and gave homage to the punk influence on fashion. They were paired with neon shirts. Wide belts also returned and chunky jewelry reminiscent of the large necklaces and earrings of the 1980s became popular again. In 2009 Ralph Lauren resurrected the 1930s for men. His collection sported suspendered slacks with "mended" tears and patches, reminiscent of real mends and patches that were necessary in the 1930s when much of the world was in a great depression. The difference, though, was in the 1930s the aesthetic was about clothing, while in 2009 it was about fashion. Today, with postmodernist pluralism influencing much of fashion, many prior trends have returned and are worn in unison: 1900s bell-shaped sleeves, 1930s backless dresses, 1940s high-waisted and wide-panted slacks, 1950s slim slacks and skinny ties, 1980s unstructured jackets with rolled sleeves and skinny ties (which in the 1980s was a homage to the 1950s), 1960s ethnic jewelry, 1970s skinny belts, 1970s peasant blouses, bellbottoms, and wedges, 1980s oversized silhouettes, ripped jeans and high waistlines, and so on.

Why does fashion history return? Some people like the memories and nostalgic feel. It may recall happy memories of their adolescence or foster the romanticized feeling of an era they are too young to remember but wish they knew. Also there are only so many ways a shirt or dress or slacks can be made or styled, so returning to the past is a good way to make something appear new, especially if it is for a new customer or market segment. Additionally, George Sproles (1985) argued that no truly new styles are created because "the human body has been decorated in every conceivable manner" (p. 62). Therefore, designers borrow from the past and reinterpret it for the current era. In addition, past fashions can be viewed as ironic (and reflect the postmodern climate) when something out-of-date is made fashionable again, such as the Nerd Chic look of the 2010s borrowing outdated fashions of the 1980s.

One reason why fashions from prior eras are revived and become popularized again is the role of nostalgia. **Nostalgia** is looking at past events or eras with a longing to return to them. Often, nostalgia invokes thinking of something in romantic or sentimental terms when times were easier. However, this glosses over the fact that often those sentimental "good old days" were rife with anxiety and their own issues. For example, the 1940s are viewed as a nostalgic time in American history when the nation banded together to fight the Japanese, German, and Italian armies. People think of the romance of Canteen dances, Rosie the Riveter, or the iconic kiss between a sailor and a woman in Times Square to celebrate the end of World War II. However, in reality, the 1940s were difficult. People were dying in war, money was tight, and food was scarce. These tend to be glossed over in nostalgia memories. Nonetheless, nostalgia tends to be a strong force in designing and acceptance of past fashions.

Branding

On a cattle ranch cows are branded using a disk of metal heated in a fire that is then burned into the cow's hide and leaves a permanent impression burned into the skin. This is done so that the cattle rancher can identify his or her stock, and also so that others can identify it as well. A fashion brand is similar, where an image is metaphorically burned into the consumer's mind. After World War II, there was an increase in ready-to-wear garments and manufacturers and designers needed a way to make their merchandise stand out from the crowd of other manufacturers and designers offering similar products. A black dress is a black dress is a black dress. They may be made by different people, use different fabrics and have a different style but in general they look the same, and in order for manufacturers to differentiate themselves they needed to create a brand. Like on a cattle ranch, the brand displays who you are as well as who you are not.[2]

Branding is not a theory but rather a concept that is important to the fashion industry. Fashion scholar Joseph Hancock (2009) wrote, "Branding is not just about individual products, but creates an identity for the company, for consumers, as well as for those who work within the organization. Branding creates a vision for the company" (p. 5). Branding allows companies to differentiate themselves from competitors of similar products. Clare McCardell was an American designer in the 1950s and 1960s who advocated for simple pieces that women could mix and match. She borrowed from or found inspiration from sportswear and made them into fashionable pieces. When Clare McCardell designed for the firm Townley, she created an A-line dress. Customers did not see the difference of this simple style and chose the cheaper competitor (Arnold, 2000). Brand recognition and brand value would have made the difference. Had Clare McCardell or Townley branded their merchandise, customers who value the brand would likely have purchased the more-expensive Clare McCardell design. Any basic or otherwise undistinguishable garment, that looks like everyone else's, needs to be branded, as well as unique products that emphasize the brand's aesthetic tastes.

Sometimes a company creates a backstory for a new brand to give it an identity. When the Abercrombie and Fitch company launched the upscale retail store Ruehl No. 925 in 2004, it manufactured a history for the company—that the Ruehl family immigrated to the United States from Germany during the middle of the 19th century and opened a leather goods shop at No. 925 Greenwich Street, Manhattan,

New York City. The story continues that the company was expanded with two successive generations to sell clothing until sold to Abercrombie and Fitch in 2002 who continue the Ruehl family tradition. Even the logo—a bulldog named Trubble—was said to be a likeness of the original owner's dog. This story is complete fiction, but it creates a brand image for the company, establishes a heritage (albeit false), and appeals to a segment of consumers who appreciate a rags-to-riches story. However, the retail concept did not do well and by 2010 all stores were closed. Nonetheless, Abercrombie and Fitch has used this method of creating a background story for its other retail concepts, including Gilly Hicks and Hollister Co.[3]

The concept of branding is important because it creates a connection between the product and the customer and differentiates one product from another. Customers become loyal to brands, which generates repeat-patronage. The image is created through advertising, promotional materials, visual display and customer's experience with the brand that align to create a specific image. A shopping experience at Abercrombie and Fitch is different from a shopping experience at Prada. The Abercrombie and Fitch store is dimly lit, loud music is played, and promotional materials include larger-than-life black and white images of (mostly) nude models. The image they are selling is hyper sexuality. In addition, Abercrombie and Fitch employees are trained to be aloof and use slang (e.g., "later" for good bye) that is synonymous with the Southern California image the brand cultivates. Meanwhile, Prada is bright with plush carpeting and no music playing. Sales people wear black suits and black knit gloves. The gloves prevent soiling of garments or fingerprints on the glittering jewelry, but they also hint at the "museum quality" of the products. In addition, they encase customers' receipts in an envelope made of stock-quality paper, which has been printed with their logo. Both Abercrombie and Fitch and Prada brands "speak" to different consumer markets and provide a specialized experience to the customers to make emotional connections with them.

According to fashion and clothing scholar Lou Taylor (2000) in the early 1990s established couture houses like Givenchy, Chloe and Dior began to re-brand and re-imagine themselves as youthful to court a newer, more lucrative market than their small number of couture customers. Marketing created the illusion of luxury. Image was paramount above all else. John Galliano made Dior into an opulent fantasy of exotic collections though extravagant fashion shows and clothing. Tom Ford made Gucci the image of jet-setting lifestyle by introducing new products (velvet slippers were one of the new products) and brushing the dust off classic handbag designs. Karl Lagerfeld made Chanel decadent and sensual by playing on established aesthetics of Chanel but exaggerating them.

One clever marketing technique of the brand is to extend the reputation of the name beyond the original products. A brand allows nearly everyone to partake in the world of luxurious goods thorough purchasing objects that are affordable. Nowhere is this truer than the luxury fragrance market. A Dior, Prada, Gucci, or Chanel ensemble may be out of range for most people, but their fragrances are comparatively a bargain. Grant McCracken (1988) calls this **_displaced meaning_**.

111

Figure 5.4 Gap quickly returned to their iconic blue and white logo after 5 days when their new logo courted backlash. Northfoto/Shutterstock.com.

By creating displaced meaning more people can partake in the brand lifestyle and in return businesses increase profits and market share.

One of the key elements of the brand is the logo. "The logo is essential to . . . success . . . Every franchised designer product bears this badge of status . . . which enables these goods to be sold far beyond their actual value" (Taylor, 2000, 137). The aesthetics of the logo provide instant recognition of not only the name but also what the name (or brand) signifies. Chanel's interlocking Cs, Gucci's interlocking Gs, and Louis Vuitton's angled LV may appear simple, but they provide a powerful, instant brand recognition and stand for more than letters stamped on a product.

When Gap changed their logo in 2010 it was met with resistance and outcry from its consumers. The old logo of a blue box with the Gap spelled in capital letters was replaced with lowercase, Helvetica font; the blue box was reduced in size and its color graded. Public outcry was enormous. The new logo was likened to logos of pharmaceutical companies and IT companies and described as boring, bland, and incongruent with the Gap brand image. Less than one week after unveiling the new logo, it was eschewed for the former one. This example illustrates the loyalty, passion, and dedication to brand and brand logo (see Figure 5.4).

BOXED CASE 5.1: ETHICS FOCUS: KNOCK-OFFS

As a designer you spend your time and money researching a trend. You spend untold hours developing the pattern, readjusting, and perfecting it. You scour the markets for the perfect fabric and you agonize over selecting the right buttons. You manufacture it and market it and are proud when it is hailed in the press as triumph. Then one week later you see a copy of it in a retail store selling for a fraction of the cost you are selling the item for, and using a different brand label. Your design has been stolen; what do you do?

Knock-offs are copies of designs and should not be confused with counterfeits. Counterfeits, while also copies, are made to fool the customer into believing they are the genuine product. Counterfeits are illegal in most countries. However, knock-offs are made to resemble another design but are sold under a different label (see Figures 5.5 and 5.6). Knock-offs may or may not be illegal, depending on the country.

In Europe, you would have recourse if your original design was deemed unique. In Europe, fashion designs are protected for 25 years from being copied and copiers can be prosecuted. However, in the United States, fashion designs are not legally protected from being copied (note: prints and logos can be protected). A major component of the United States fashion system is the knock-off industry and some argue that (a) knock-offs help promote a trend, and (b) the economy would crash without knock-offs. However, designers argue that their hard work has been usurped and competitors are making money from their hard work. Lobbying groups such as the Council of Fashion Designers of America are arguing for legal protection and currently there is potential legislation in the United States that could protect unique designs for three years.

One designer, Rose (not her real name, she wished to remain anonymous for this publication), said she no longer produces mass quantities especially for this reason. Rose said that in the early 1990s she had a line of ladies' casual clothing and one dress had a very distinctive design, both in pattern and in construction. She sold to retail stores and one day she went into one of the retail stores to find that her dress was no longer on the mannequins, but a copy of it was. Rose looked at the tag and saw that it was now made in Asia and under the store's private label. She said she looked into taking the retailer to court but the costs would have outweighed the result. Today, Rose makes small quantities with limited distributions. She sells directly to the consumer and bypasses the retailer. Unfortunately, situations like this are not isolated.

Figure 5.5 Dominique Maitre/WWD © Condé Nast 2009.

Figure 5.6 The unique design of the Hermès Birkin bag (5.5) has spawned many knock-offs (5.6). Josephine Schiele/Lucky © Condé Nast.

BOXED CASE 5.2: NEW TECHNOLOGY OF BODY FASHIONS

A **cyborg** is a being with technological parts graphed or merged into its original body. They are widely featured in science-fiction literature, television shows, film, and animation, and for many years have been the idea of fancy. Yet, as body modifications are becoming more fashionable and technology is advancing, some people are becoming cyborgs. Products are being implanted onto and into the human body to improve its function, while at the same time also changing its aesthetics. Below are four novel ways that technology is changing people into cyborgs.

- Pierced eyeglasses: Earrings and body piercings are common, but James Sooy's new design for eyewear is truly revolutionary. The lenses are attached to metal hinges that are then pierced to the bridge of the nose. No need for the eyeglass arms anymore.
- QR tattoos: The rectangular QR code is tattooed onto skin and when read by a smartphone's QR code reader, it links to a website. The contents of the website can be changed as frequently as desired, so that the tattoo is continually "evolving" or "updated."
- Magnetic fingers: Magnets are implanted into fingertips so they can easily pick up magnetized parts.
- Skin cellphones: Jim Mielke has created a touch screen that can be implanted under skin. The device uses a special type of dye so that when a person receives a call a digital image of the person calling appears on the skin. When the call ends, the image disappears from the skin. How does it run? Not on batteries; it runs on blood (thus making it environmentally friendly).

Summary

The fashion system plays a vital role in the life of fashion and trends. Decisions that designers, merchandisers, marketers, forecasters, and retailers make affect what becomes a trend and what does not become a trend. Some fashions exist because they were the only available styles in a marketplace and some styles become fashions because companies have made them available at different price points simultaneously to different markets. But the importance of technological innovation, branding, and history cannot be overlooked because they play a role in what can be produced and how it will be received or perceived by the public.

Key Terms

- Better
- Branding
- Bridge
- Budget
- Cyborg
- Designer
- Innovation theory
- Knock-offs

- La Chambre Syndicale de la Couture
- Displaced meaning
- Gatekeeper
- Haute couture
- Historic resurrection

- Market infrastructure theory
- Mere exposure hypothesis
- Moderate
- Nostalgia
- Trickle across theory

Discussion questions

1. Why do fashion designers look to the past for inspiration? Why cannot they come up with something new?
2. What nostalgic trends do you observe in fashion now?
3. What technological innovation has impacted your aesthetic style?
4. Would you have a cellphone implanted in your arm?
5. What gatekeepers of fashion hold the most power?

Learning activities

1. Research a company with many different brands (e.g., Burberry). Find images or examples of the different lines and analyze what design features, marketing, and price points make them different from each other.
2. You will need access to an historic costume collection for this activity. Find examples of garments that used technology new at the time (e.g., a new fiber, a new way of construction, a new item like a zipper). Note how the invention made dressing easier, if at all. Discuss if this invention revolutionized fashion or was just briefly influential. Is it still being used today or has it changed with additional technological advances?

───────── Notes ─────────

1. As noted in Chapter 1 there are many different fashion systems in the world. However, this chapter will focus on the western fashion system given the intended audience of this text.

2. The first widely recognized brand was Coca-Cola. Established in the 1880s, the marketing scheme encouraged people to ask for a Coca-Cola by name, rather than simply asking for a cola which at the time was common.

3. Gilly Hick's fictional background is that she was young British woman who studied in Paris and moved to Sydney, Australia to open an underwear retail store in 1932. Hollister Co.'s fictional background is that John Hollister, Sr., moved from New York to purchase a rubber plantation in the Dutch East Indies before opening a store in 1922 in California.

───────── Further reading ─────────

Cline, E. L. (2012). *Overdressed: The Shockingly High Cost of Cheap Fashion*. New York City: Portfolio/Penguin.

Gomez-Aubert, C. (2011). New rules for old gems: Can El Salvador sustain and develop home grown design? *Textile: The Journal of Cloth and Culture, 9* (3), 288–307.

Leopold, E. (1992). The manufacture of the fashion system. In J. Ash and E. Wilson (eds) *Chic Thrills: A Fashion Reader*. London: Pandora.

McCracken, G. (1988). *Culture and Consumption*. Bloomington, Indiana: Indiana University Press.

Miller, M. S. (2008/2009). Piracy in our backyard: A comparative analysis of the implications of fashion copyrighting in the United States for the International Copyright Community. *Journal of International Media and Entertainment Law, 2*, pp. 133–158.

Richardson, P. (2013). Tips for working in luxury sales. In K. Miller-Spillman, A. Reilly, and P. Hunt-Hurst, *The Meanings of Dress 3rd edition* (pp. 69–71). New York City: Fairchild Books.

6

CONCLUSION

Up until the mid-20th century fashion could be explained by a handful of theories. These theories constituted a modern perspective on fashion. Chief among them was the Trickle Down theory, but historic resurrection, historic continuity, and shifting erogenous zones were also insightful and helped to explain why fashions changed. But, by the middle of the 20th century, the examination of fashion required new explanations. The new fashion process disrupted the expected course of fashion. No longer did designers have absolute sway over trends where a desire to change a hemline or advocate for a new color would mean everyone followed suit. No longer could Dior, Givenchy, Balenciaga, Balmain and others dictate silhouettes, patterns, colors, and hemlines based on their desires for the season. As we look back at fashion history, during the early part of the 20th century and before, there were only a few defining looks. However, to be fair, Valerie Steele (1998) has argued, "Couturiers like Worth, Chanel, and Dior were not so much dictators or radical innovators as they were astute barometers of fashion trends" (p. 5). By the end of the 20th century, there was a multiplicity of defining looks. Fashion had changed—but how and why?

Valerie Steele (2000) argued that, "As the haute couture was transformed from a system based on the atelier to one dominated by the global corporate conglomerate, Paris was the capital of fashion, but its mode of influence owed much to American-style licensing and mass-manufacturing" (p. 8). During World War II while Paris was under siege, London blitzed, and other European capitals of fashion struggling for survival, the American fashion system took precedence. American designers like Claire McCardell, Bonnie Cashin, and Anne Klein introduced new ideas like sportswear and coordinating separates. After World War II ended the Paris fashion scene bounced back with Dior's magnificent and revolutionary New Look in 1947. But new concepts of designing, conducting business, and social groups were taking root. The Trickle Down theory began to lose predictive power with the advent of mass production, when it was observed the upper strata were no longer starting all fashion trends (Blumer 1969; Lowe & Lowe 1985).

New theories were emerging to explain the new face of fashion. The Trickle Up theory, Collective Behavior theory, and the concepts of branding and mass marketing offered new explanations for fashion change in the postmodern era. Fashion was becoming more democratic in the sense that it was not the privilege of the wealthy, but now fashion could be enjoyed by all classes. Perhaps the greatest example of democratic fashion is found in denim jeans; born from the working class, fostered by rebellion, it has become a near-universal mode of dress. To meet the new emerging markets, and differentiate one manufacturer from another, branding became vital to success. Branding focused on lifestyles and sought out niche-markets. Fashion was becoming even bigger business.

By the 21st century many of the dominating luxury houses were owned by conglomerates. LVMH amassed Louis Vuitton, Fendi, Thomas Pink, Marc Jacobs, Donna Karan, Kenzo, and Celine as well as perfume companies Parfums Christian Dior, Guerlain, and Acqua di Parma, jewelry companies like Tag Heuer, and retail companies like DFS, La Bon Marche, and Sephora. Meanwhile PPR bought Gucci, Bottega Venetta, Balenciaga, Brioni, Christopher Kane, and partially owns Alexander McQueen and Stella McCartney. A corporate strategy to the business of fashion had taken root.

As we move into the post-postmodern era, new theories will emerge to explain new looks and new fashions. Morgado's (in press) work on post-postmodernism is perhaps the first analysis of this era on fashion. No doubt, some theories will fail to explain new trends, some will be modified, and some new theories will be developed. Even fashion theories can go in and out of fashion.

One phenomenon, many theories

While reading this text you may have realized that a phenomenon (i.e., fashion trend) can be explained by more than one theory. You read that irezumi can be explained by subcultural style and spatial diffusion; it was an aesthetic of the Yakuza of Japan and therefore by default geographically located to specifics areas of Japan. The same came be said of Mods, whose 1960s modern style was both a feature of a youthful subculture as well as of London. The same can also be said of Hippies, whose organic style was a subculture at one time specific to San Francisco. The trend and popularity of the leisure suit is also explained by at least two theories. The invention of polyester created a new fiber for designers to use (Innovation theory), was different from prior versions of the man's suit (uniqueness), originally was expensive but price decreased with availability (supply and demand), and reflected to the times of the era (Zeitgeist). Backless dresses, popular in the 1980s, can be explained by historic resurrection (they were popular in the 1930s) as well as shifting erogenous zones. Thus, a fashion trend can have more than one explanation based on the context or the "lens" through which the phenomenon is examined: psychological, social, cultural, or industrial. Using Hamilton's continuum you can analyze events at different macro and micro levels in order to gain a full understanding of the situation.

Dorothy Behling (1985/1986) combined the trickle up and trickle down theories into one model and demonstrated how the median age of the population played a factor—fashion trickles up when the median age of the population is youthful, and fashion trickles down when the median age of the population is older. Hence, whichever age group is most populous during a given time, they serve as the fashion innovators and fashion inspiration. However, Behling does note that the economy and government regulations can disrupt the model.

Additionally the theories of the historic continuity and shifting erogenous zones can explain the same phenomenon. When a new erogenous zone is revealed it may coincide with a new trend that is also explained by historic continuity. By early 2013, the lengths of pants were starting to decrease, so that the hem hit just above the ankle. One explanation is that pants length had reached their maximum endpoint and needed to reverse direction. Another explanation is that the ankle was the new sexy. In the early 2010s, American retail brand Old Navy promoted "high-water" pants by encouraging customers to "show those sexy ankles."

As you continue on with your education and begin your career in fashion, this is important to remember. Before you make any decision, you need to remember to analyze a situation from all perspectives. By linking two or more theories, you will have a better understanding of the trend and a better platform from which to make your choices.

Fashion blunders

Of course, not all attempts at creating new products and styles are successful, even if they were based on sound reasoning. Some companies that have tried to create a new fashion trend have failed and become lessons for others. In this book you have seen the example of Halston and Gucci. Halston's and Gucci's falls were due to overexposure as well as losing sight of the importance of the brand. Both labels were highly valued by consumers when they were considered exclusive, but when the name was found on products offered at lower prices, their loyal clientele found no more value in the brand. You also read about the Gap's failed attempt to change its logo, which illustrated the company either did not understand the power of its logo or the loyalty of its clients. Following are other examples of fashion blunders.

John Fairchild and the midi

The mini-skirt was made popular in London during the 1960s. Though the design has been credited to Mary Quant, André Courrèges, and Barbara Hulanicki, in fact the mini was worn on the streets before any branded designers trimmed their skirt lengths above the knee; however, they did help popularize it among different markets. It became a staple feature of the youthful London Mods and was a fashion staple through the remainder of the decade.

John Fairchild was the publisher/owner/editor of the popular and powerful trade publication *Women's Wear Daily*. He wielded a lot of power in the press and apparently thought he wielded a lot of power in the fashion process too. In 1970 he declared the mini-skirt dead and that the calf-length midi-skirt would take its place in women's wardrobes. He vigorously promoted the midi-skirt and given Fairchild's prominence and influence in the fashion industry, buyers, designers, manufacturers, and retailers followed his advice. The result was a disaster. Consumers did not want a longer skirt and protested. Some wore "Stop the Midi" pins on their lapels. *Time* magazine even covered the travesty on September 14, 1970 with the cover story, "John Fairchild of *Women's Wear Daily:* The Man Behind the Midi Mania." The article reported protests and petitions to bring the mini-skirt back on the market. The article also reported the president of the Association for Buying Offices accused *Women's Wear Daily* of killing the fall and spring season for manufacturers. Dress scholar Marcia Morgado (personal communication, 2013) recalled that many people lost their business as a result of following Fairchild's advice.

While the Market Infrastructure theory surmises that only products sold in stores can become fashion, it overlooks two key concepts. First, John Fairchild lost sight that that fashion system had changed—fashion trend was no longer dictated by a few people; it was dictated by the masses and trends could not be pushed on them. Second, he also lost sight of the fact that fashion changes slowly; as noted by the theory of historic continuity, abrupt changes are not digestible.

Tommy Hilfiger and the high-end market

Hilfiger was once a hugely popular brand and a true rival of Ralph Lauren's Polo label in the 1980s and early 1990s; then in the late 1990s, Hilfiger lost its stance. According to Lou Taylor (2000) Hilfiger's failure was that the brand went from middle class to high-end, when the opposite is what normally worked for businesses. Hilfiger began as a ready-to-wear brand that was marketed and promoted so successfully that it quickly became legendary. His marketing scheme was to create the illusion that his mass-market clothes were status (i.e., designer) clothes by co-opting the same techniques couture houses had used. He was extremely successful in the youth market and the emerging hip-hop scene where his clothes were seen as status symbols. Then he opted to open a truly high-end store and expand his brand to sell exclusive, designer products made of luxury textiles like cashmere. The venture failed. Taylor argued that, even if his designs were not on par with other high-end brands, the momentum from mass market to luxury was the contrary to the usual marketing strategy of luxury to mass market.

Ungaro and Lindsay Lohan

The once-influential fashion house of Ungaro wanted to revive its brand and hired actress Lindsay Lohan as artistic director. The unveiling of a 2009 Lohan-inspired Ungaro collection was met with ridicule and disastrous reviews by the media and customers. Lohan left the company a year later. In theory, hiring a celebrity is a good idea because of the influence and clout the celebrity wields. However, the choice of Lindsay Lohan was peculiar given her limited work in the fashion industry, recent string of bad publicity, and arrests for drug and alcohol abuse. There are two lessons to be learned from this situation: (1) if you are going to hire a celebrity designer be sure s/he understands the nature of fashion; a lot can be forgiven (bad press, arrests) but bad design is not one of them; and (2) be sure your celebrity has the talent to inspire others and create saleable products.

Hypercolor

In 1991, Generra Sportswear Company marketed Hypercolor t-shirts. These shirts were made of fabric that changed color when exposed to heat. In theory this innovation sounds like a great inspiration for fashion—a shirt that changes color when you walk outside would be quite outstanding, eye-catching, and if marketed well would be quite popular. However, Hypercolor t-shirts had a short lifespan in the market. When worn, body areas that generated heat, such as the underarms, generated unwanted attention through the change of color. The result was the appearance of a sweaty mess. This error of judgment illustrates that not all innovations are adaptable to fashion products.

Princesses Eugenie's and Beatrice's hats

In 2011, British Princesses Eugenie and Beatrice attended the wedding of Kate Middleton to Prince William. Royalty typically have been fashion icons; Kate Middleton had established herself as a fashion communicator, as had the late Princess Diana. However, Eugenie and Beatrice's peculiar hats garnered the wrong type of attention, when the media and wedding watchers criticized the chapeaux designed by Philip Treacy (see Figure 6.1). Some people argued it was in bad taste to wear something so unusual to a dignified ceremony. The hats may have been better received on the runway than at a royal wedding. The lesson to learn here is to understand the context in which a new design will be worn.

Figure 6.1 Princesses Eugenie and Beatrice of York were ridiculed by viewers and press for the peculiar hats they wore to the wedding of Prince William and Catherine Middleton. Pascal Le Segretain/Getty Images.

BOXED CASE 6.1: ETHICS FOCUS: OFFENSIVE FASHION

While fashion can be fun and exciting, there are times when fashions can be offensive to people. They can offend the group of people that inspired the fashion trend or they can be offensive due to the use of historically reprehensible icons and motifs.

Many fashion trends can trace their roots to ethnic or religious groups. Rosaries come from the Catholic faith, kabala bracelets from the Jewish faith, moccasins from Native Americans, ponchos from Mexico, tattoos from Polynesia, and so forth. Yet, due to the disposable nature of fashion, borrowing or finding inspiration from ethnic and religious groups can be ethically problematic. In Polynesia, tattoos are given as a rite of passage to indicate status. In Southeast Asia the bindi (colored dot between the eyebrows) is a religious symbol of wisdom and protection. Among the Akan of Africa, kente is sacred cloth with symbolic colors and weavings. And the checkered keffiyeh scarf is a symbol of Palestinian nationalism (see Figure 6.2). However, when these items—and many others—are worn as

Figure 6.2   When the keffiyeh scarf, a traditional garment of Arab people and a symbol of Palestinian nationalism, was adopted by the broader public, it became a controversial fashion item. Vishstudio/Shutterstock.com.

125

fashion it loses its cultural significance, is viewed as costume, and offends the originating group.

Some designers find inspiration from controversial groups, such as the Hate Couture trend. Hate Couture incorporates elements of the Nazi regime or Ku Klux Klan into fashion, such as armbands with the Nazi swastika, Nazi uniforms, and shoes with the swastika on the sole (so that they leave the impression in the ground). The trend even reached celebrities and couture fashion; in 1995 the fashion house of Jean-Louis Scherrer (designed by Bernard Perris) showed couture pieces with Nazi insignia;[1] in 2005 Prince Harry of England wore a Nazi armband to a costume party and in 2006 Rocky Mazzilli offered a couture ensemble with a prominent swastika on the skirt. Elsewhere, Nazi fashion has become popular among Harajuku trendsetters. Elements of the United States Deep South can also be seen as offensive to some people. The Confederate flag is a source of controversy (some view it as racist whereas others view it as heritage) and is featured on t-shirts, shoes, bathing suits, and so forth. Meanwhile, in 2012 the Ku Klux Klan distinctive robes inspired Ivaek Archer of Chiz'l Menswear to reveal a men's robe with hoodie in the shape of the Ku Klux Klan's pointed hood, while in 2012 Rei Kawakubo showed a wedding ensemble with pointed hood at Paris fashion week.[2]

BOXED CASE 6.2: CLASSICS CAN HAVE FASHIONABLE DETAILS TOO

At the beginning of this text you read that fashions were different from fads and classic, and while this is true, there is one caveat that you should understand. Classics can have *fashionable* components to them. The little black dress is considered a classic of fashion, with its lineage dating back to Coco Chanel in the 1920s, but details such as ruffles, neckline, hemline, and silhouette have changed depending on the Zeitgeist. Likewise, Converse shoes have a classic silhouette, but the choice of color, print (e.g., solid, stripe, camouflage), and fabrication (e.g., canvas, leather) can vary with a trend (see Figure 6.3). The trench coat is also considered a classic, with Thomas Burberry claiming invention in 1901. The style has remained relatively unchanged for over a century, but details such as colors, fabrications, hem lengths, sleeve style, and buttons have changed to align with fashionable movements. The example in Figure 6.4 illustrates and demonstrates fashionable elements. In addition to their fabrication (cotton twill, wax-coated nylon, and fine merino wool) the cuffs vary with a curved, pointed, or nonexistent sleeve band. Thus, although there are some items of dress that are deemed "unchangeable," in reality there are little changes that belie the influence of fashion.

Figure 6.3 Converse shoes, considered a classic, often have fashionable elements that change, like color and print. Natali Glado/Shutterstock.com.

Figure 6.4 Details from three trench coats show the influence of fashion on a classic item of dress. Trench coats courtesy of author.

Summary

"The role of theory is to simplify what is known (codification of knowledge) and to identify what is not known (and thus, to establish logical directions for subsequent research)" (Laughlin, 1997, p. 162). Fashion theories and concepts are used by all positions in the fashion industries: apparel designers, jewelry designers, fabric designers, merchandisers, stylists, journalists, critics, forecasters, buyers, retailers, product developers, colorists, etc. Their understanding of the fashion process helps them to understand prior fashion successes (and failures) and plan for future lines and collections. They observe street cultures, track celebrities, measure hemlines, analyze the Zeitgeist, identify new technologies, understand the interaction between people and society, source rare materials, search for neighborhoods with distinctive styles, examine past fashions, and select what to design, promote, and sell at what price points.

If you choose not to use theoretical constructs in your line of work you may have some success but you will be ignoring fundamental principles of the nature of fashion. Some people may believe that fashion has no logic and that popularity of an item is purely happenstance. However, after reading this text you should realize this is not true. Theories, principles, and constructs help the professional to make wise and informed choices based on reason and logic.

Discussion questions

1. Of the theories discussed in this text, which ones do you think are the most important? Justify your response with examples.
2. When does ethnic fashion become offensive?
3. Can a theory ever "die" or not be useful anymore?

Learning activities

1. Using a fashion curve with the respective adoption categories (fashion innovators, fashion leaders, early adopters, late adopters, and fashion laggards) identify where each of the theories discussed in this text would fit. Note: A theory may be used in more than one adoption category.
2. Create your own theory of fashion. Use examples to illustrate your theory. How would you test your theory?
3. Interview a professional in the field of fashion. Ask this person how s/he uses theory in their work and which theories they find most helpful.
4. Bring in an item of clothing from your wardrobe. Discuss with the class the theory behind its design and promotion.
5. Combine two or more theories to explain a phenomenon of fashion.

Notes

1. The collection was shown during the 50th anniversary of the liberating of Auschwitz (Finkelstein, 1998).

2. Rei Kawakubo is no stranger to controversy. In 1995, also during the 50th anniversary of the liberation of Auschwitz, her Comme des Garçons collection featured fashion designs resembling concentration camp pajamas (Finkelstein, 1998).

Further reading

Agins, T. (2000). *The End of Fashion: How Marketing Changed the Clothing Business Forever*. New York City: HarperCollins.

Bikhchandani, S., Hirshleifer, D., & Welch, I. (1992). A theory of fads, fashion, custom, and cultural change as informational cascades. *Journal of Political Economy, 100* (5), 992, 10–26.

González, A. M. (2010). On fashion and fashion discourses. *Critical Studies in Fashion and Beauty 1* (1), pp. 65–84.

Neville, E. (2013). Feather hair extensions: Fashion without compassion. In K. Miller-Spillman, A. Reilly, and P. Hunt-Hurst, *The Meanings of Dress 3rd edition* (pp. 588–589). New York City: Fairchild Books.

Vincent, S. J. (2010). *The Anatomy of Fashion: Dressing the Body from the Renaissance to Today*. Oxford: Berg.

Workman, J. E. (2004). Alcohol promotional clothing items and alcohol use by university students. *Analyses of Social Issues and Public Policy, 4* (1), 69–89.

BIBLIOGRAPHY

Akihiko Izukura (n.d.). Philosophy. Downloaded April 30, 2013 from http://www.akihikoizukura.com/

Anorexia Bulimia Care (n.d.). Information and statistics. Downloaded May 27, 2013 from http://www.anorexiabulimiacare.org.uk/information-and-statistics-media

Arnold, R. (2000). Luxury and restraint: Minimalism in 1990s fashion. In N. White & I. Griffiths, (eds) *The Fashion Business: Theory, Practice, Image* (pp. 167–182). Oxford: Berg.

Arthur, L. (2000). *Aloha Attire: Hawaiian Dress in the Twentieth Century*. Atglen, PA: Schiffer.

Arthur, L. B. (1997). Cultural authentication refined: The case of the Hawaiian Holoku. *Clothing and Texiltes Research Journal, 15* (3), 129–139.

Arthur, L. B. (2008). East meets west: The aloha shirt as an instrument of acculturation. In A. Reilly & S. Cosbey (eds) *The Men's Fashion Reader* (pp. 295–310). New York: Fairchild Books.

Aune, R. Kelly. (1999). The effects of perfume use on perceptions of attractiveness and competence. In L. K. Guerrero, J. A. DeVito, & M. L. Hecht (eds) *The Nonverval Communication Reader: Classic and Contemporary Readings* (second edition; pp. 126–132). Prospect Heights, Illinois: Waveland Press, Inc.

Baardwijk, van, M., & Franses P. H. (2010). The hemline and the economy: Is there any match? Econometric Institute Report 2010–40. Rotterdam, the Netherlands: Erasmus University. Downloaded May 1, 2013 from http://repub.eur.nl/res/pub/20147/EI%202010-40.pdf

Babbie, E. (2004). *The Practice of Social Research* (10th edition). Belmont, California: Wadsworth/Thompson Learning.

Behling, D. (1985/1986). Fashion change and demographics: A model. *Clothing and Textiles Research Journal, 4* (1), 18–23.

Benjamin, W. (2003). *Selected Writings, Volume IV, 1938–1940*. Trans Edmund Jephcott et al., ed. Howard Eiland and Michael W. Jennings. Cambridge, Massachusetts: Belknap Press of Harvard University.

Blumer, H. (1962). Society as symbolic interaction. In A. M. Rose (ed.) *Human Behavior and Social Process: An Interactionist Approach* (pp. 179–192). London: Houghton-Mifflin.

Blumer, H. (1968). Fashion. *International Encyclopedia of the Social Sciences V.* New York: Macmillan.

Blumer, H. (1969). Fashion: From class differentation to collective selection. *Sociological Quarterly, 10*, 275–291.

Boehn, M. (1932). *Modes and Manner* (Vols. I–IV). London, George G. Harrap.

Bourdieu, P. (1984). *Distinction: A Social Critique of Judgment of Taste*. London: Routledge and Kegan Paul.

Bourdieu, P. (1990). Structures, habitus, practices. In P. Bordieu, *The Logic of Practice* (pp. 52–79). Stanford, California: Stanford University Press.

Boucher, F. (1987). *20,000 Years of Fashion: The History of Costume and Personal Adornment*. New York: Harry N. Abrams, Inc.

Bourriaud, N. (2009). *Altermodern*. London: Tate Publishing.

Brannon, E. L. (2005). *Fashion Forecasting* (2nd edition). New York: Fairchild Publications, Inc.

Brook, T. (1999). *The Confusions of Pleasure: Commerce and Culture in Ming China*. Berkeley and Los Angeles, California: University of California Press.

Cannon, A. (1998). The cultural and historical contents of fashion. In A. Bryden & S. Niessen (eds) *Consuming Fashion: Adorning the Transnational Body* (pp. 23–38). Oxford: Berg.

Clements, K. (2013). *The Vogue Factor: From Front Desk to Editor*. Melbourne, Australia: Melbourne University Publishing.

Christopher, C. (2012). Skin bleaching: The complexion of identity, beauty, and fashion. In K. Spillman-Miller, A. Reilly, & P. Hunt-Hurst (eds), *Meanings of Dress* 3rd edition (pp. 154–160). New York: Fairchild Books.

Craik, J. (1994). *The Face of Fashion: Cultural Studies in Fashion*. New York: Routledge.

Craik, J. (2009). *Fashion: The Key Concepts*. Oxford: Berg.

Curran, L. (1999). An Analysis of Cycles in Skirt Lengths and Widths in the UK and Germany, 1954–1990. *Clothing and Textiles Research Journal, 17* (2), 65–72.

Curry, D. (1993). Decorating the Body Politic. *New Formations 19*: 69–82

d'Errico, F., Henshilwood, C., Vanhaeren, M., & van Niekerk, K. (2005). *Nassarius kraussianus* Shell Beads from Blombos Cave: Evidence for Symbolic Behavior in the Middle Stone Age. *Journal of Human Evolution*, 48 (1), 3–24.

Dalby, L. (1993). *Kimono: Fashioning Culture*. New Haven, Connecticut: Yale University Press.

Damhorst, M. L. (1989, July 16–18). Contextual model of clothing sign system. Presentation made at the *Colloquium on the Body and Clothing as Communication, International Institute of Marketing Meaning*. Indianapolis, Indiana, USA.

Damhorst, M. L. (2005). Dress as nonverbal communication. In M. L. Damhorst, K. A. Miller-Spillman, & S. O. Michelman (eds), *Meanings of Dress* 2nd edition (pp. 67–80). New York: Fairchild.

Davenport, M. (1976). *The Book of Costume*. New York: Crown Publishers, Inc.

Davis, F. (1982). On the "symbolic" in symbolic interaction. *Symbolic Interactionism, 5*, 111–126.

DeLong, M. R. (1998). *The Way We Look: Dress and Aesthetics*. New York City: Fairchild.

Delong, M., & Park, J. (2008). From cool to hot to cool: The case for the black leather jacket. In A. Reilly & S. Cosbey (eds) *Men's Fashion Reader* (pp. 166–179). New York: Fairchild.

Dorey, F. (2013). "Homo sapiens – modern humans". Accessed November 27, 2013 from http://australianmuseum.net.au/Homo-sapiens-modern-humans/

Downey, L. (2009). The invention of Levi's ® 501 ® Jeans. Available from the author LDowney@levi.com, Levi Strauss & Company, San Francisco, California.

Driscoll, C. (2010). Chanel: The order of things. *Fashion Theory, 14* (2), 135–158.

Druesedow, J. L. (2010). Snapshot: Amish, Mennonites, Hutterites, and Brethren, In J. B. Eicher (ed.) *Berg Encyclopedia of World Dress and Fashion. Volume 3* (pp. 496–498). Oxford: Berg.

Dwyer, R. (2000). Bombay ishtyle. In S. Bruzzi & P. C Gibson (eds) *Fashion Cultures: Theories, Explorations and Analysis* (pp. 178–190). London: Routledge.

Dwyer, R., & Patel, D. (2002). *Cinema India: The Visual Culture of Indian Cinema*. New Brunswick, New Jersey: Rutgers University Press.

Eicher, J. B. (1981). Influences of changing resources on clothing, textiles, and the quality of life: Dressing for reality, fun, and fantasy. *Combined Proceedings, Eastern, Central, and Western Regional Meetings of Association of College Professors of Textiles and Clothing, Inc.*, pp. 36–41.

Eicher, J. B. (2004). A ping-pong example of cultural authentication and Kalabari cut-thread. *Textile Society of America 9th Biennial Symposium* proceedings. Downloaded May 1, 2013 from http://digitalcommons.unl.edu/tsaconf/439/

Eicher, J. B., & Erekosima, T. V. (1980). Distinguishing non-western from western dress: The concept of cultural authentication. *Proceedings of the 1980 Annual Meeting of the Association of College Professors of Textiles and Clothing* (pp. 83–84).

Eicher, J. B., & Erekosima, T. V. (1995). Why do they call it Kalabari? Authentication and the demarcation of ethnic identity. In J. B. Eicher (ed.) *Dress and Ethnicity* (pp. 139–164). Oxford: Berg.

Eicher J. B., & Miller, K. A. (1994). Dress and the public, private and secret self: Revisiting a model. *ITAA Proceedings*, Proceedings of the International Textile and Apparel Association, Inc., p. 145.

Entwistle, J. (2008). From catwalk to catalog: Male fashion models, masculinity, and identity. In A. Reilly & S. Cosbey (eds), *The Men's Fashion Reader* (pp. 126–144). New York: Fairchild.

Erekosima, T., V., & Eicher, J. B. (1981). Kalabari cut-thread and pulled-thread cloth: An example of cultural authentication. *African Arts, 14* (2), 48–51, 81.

Eschelman, E. (2000–2001). Performatism, or the end of postmodernism. *Anthropoetics, 6* (2).

Field, G. A. (1970). The status float phenomenon. *Business Horizons, 8*, 45–52.

Finkelstein, J. (1998). *Fashion: An Introduction*. New York City: New York Universtiy Press.

Fischer, G. V. (2001). *Pantaloons and Power: A Nineteenth-Century Dress Reform in the United States*. Kent, Ohio: The Kent State University Press.

Flugel, J. C. (1930). *The Psychology of Clothes*. London: Hogarth Press.

Forden, S. G. (2001). *The House of Gucci: A Sensations Story of Murder, Madness, Glamour, and Greed*. New York City: HarperCollins.

Freud, S. (1995). *The Basic Writings of Sigmund Freud (Psychopathology of Everyday Life, The Interpretation of Dreams, and Three Contributions to the Theory of Sex)* (A. A. Brill, ed., & A. A. Brill, trans.). New York: Random House.

Frith, H., & Gleeson, K. (2004). Clothing and embodiment: Men managing body image and appearance. In K. Miller-Spillman, A. Reilly & P. Hunt-Hurst (eds) *Meanings of Dress* 3rd edition (pp. 142–151). New York: Fairchild Books.

Fruesdow, J. L. (2010). Snapshot: Amish, Mennonites, Hutterites, and Brethren. In P. Tortora (ed.), *Berg Encyclopedia of World Dress and Fashion: The United States and Canada* (pp. 496–498). Oxford: Berg.

Gaulme, D., & Gaulme, F. (2012). *Power & Style: A World History of Politics and Dress* (trans. Deke Dusinberre). Paris, Flammarion.

GalileoSmith (2010, July 14). Response to chat room thread "Are tank tops & 'wife beater' tshirts low class?" Downloaded January 4, 2013 from http://www.city-data.com/forum/fashion-beauty/1030748-tank-tops-wife-beater-tshirts-low.html

Geller, A. C., Colditz, G., Oliveria, S., Emmons, K., Jorgensen, C., Aweh, G. N., & Frazier, A. L. (2002). Use of sunscreen, sunburning rates, and tanning bed use among more than 10,000 US children and adolescents. *Pediatrics, 109* (6), 1009–1014.

Gladwell, M. (2002). *The Tipping Point: How Little Things Can Make a Big Difference*. New York: Back Bay Books/Little, Brown and Co.

Goldfarb, M. (2013, April 4). Class calculator: A US view of the class system. *BBC News Magazine*. Downloaded April 9, 2013 from http://www.bbc.co.uk/news/magazine-22025328?print=true

Gordon, M. (2012). Personal communication.

Grogan, S. (2008). *Body Image: Understanding Body Dissatisfaction in Men, Women, and Children*. East Sussex, United Kingdom: Routledge.

Guenther, I. (2004). *Nazi Chic? Fashioning Women in the Third Reich*. Oxford: Berg Publishers.

Hamilton, J. A. (1997). The macro-micro interface in the construction of individual fashion forms and meanings. *Clothing and Textiles Research Journal, 15* (3), 164–171.

Hancock, J. (2009). *Brand/Story: Ralph, Vera, Johnny, Billy and Other Adventures in Fashion Branding*. New York: Fairchild Books.

Hartman, D. (2011, October 8–9). The gentleman adventurer. *The Wall Street Journal*, pp. D1–D2.

Henshilwood, C. S., d'Errico, F., Yates, R., Jacobs, Z., Tribolo, C., Duller, G. A. T., Mercier, N., Sealy, J. C., Valladas, H., Watts, I., & Wintle, A. G. (2002) Emergence of Modern Human Behavior: Middle Stone Age Engravings from South Africa. *Science*, 295, 1278–1280.

Henshilwood, C. S., d'Errico, F. & Watts, I. (2009) Engraved ochres from the Middle Stone Age levels at Blombos Cave, South Africa. *Journal of Human Evolution*, 57, 27–47.

Hoffecker, J., & Scott, J. (2002, March 21). *Excavations In Eastern Europe Reveal Ancient Human Lifestyles*, University of Colorado at Boulder News Archive.

Hoffmann, K. A. (2012). Perrault's "Cendrillon" among the glass tales: Crystal fantasies and glassworks in seventeenth-century France and Italy. Presentation made at Cinderella as Text of Culture conference (November 8–12, 2012).

Hooper, W. (1915). The Tudor sumptuary laws. *The English Historical Review*, 30(19), 433–449.

Hunt, A. (1996). *Governance of the Consuming Passions: A History of Sumptuary Law*. New York: St. Martin's Press.

Hyllegard, K. H., Yan, R., Ogle, J. P., & Lee, K. (2012). Socially responsible labeling: The impact of hang tags on consumers' attitudes and patronage intentions towards an apparel brand. *Clothing and Textiles Research Journal*, 30 (1), 51–66.

Jirousek, C. A. (1997). From "traditional" to "mass fashion system" dress among men in a Turkish village. *Clothing and Textiles Research Journal*, 15 (4), 203–215.

Kaiser, S. (1990). *The Social Psychology of Clothing*. New York: Macmillan.

Kaiser, S. (1997). *The Social Psychology of Clothing*. 2nd edition. New York: Fairchild.

Kaiser, S. B., Nagasawa, R. H., & Hutton, S. S. (1995). Construction of an SI theory of fashion: Part 1. Ambivalence and change. *Clothing and Textiles Research Journal*, 13 (3), 172–183.

Kaiser, S. B., Nagasawa, R. H., & Hutton, S. S. (1997). Truth, knowledge, new clothes: Responses to Hamilton, Kean, and Pannabecker. *Clothing and Textiles Research Journal*, 15 (3), 184–191.

Kanfer, S. (1993). *The Last Empire: DeBeers, Diamonds, and the World*. London: Hodder and Stoughton.

Kastanakis, M. N., & Balabanis, G. (2012). The three faces of conspicuous consumption: To belong, to differ, to out spend. *Conference Proceedings* (pp. 2638–2642). Global Marketing Conference at Seoul.

Kean, R. (1997). The role of the fashion system in fashion change: A response to the Kaiser, Nagasawa and Hutton Model. *Clothing and Textiles Research Journal*, 15 (3), 172–177.

Kerlinger, F. N. (1979). *Behavioral Research: A Conceptual Approach*. New York: Holt, Rinehart & Winston.

Kim, H., Lee, E., & Hur, W. (2012). The normative social influence on eco-friendly consumer behavior: The moderating effect of environmental marketing claims. *Clothing and Textile Research Journal*, 3(1), 4–18.

Kirby, A. (2009). *Digimodernism: How New Technologies Dismantle the Postmodern and Reconfigure Our Culture*. New York: Continuum International Publishing Group.

Ko, D. (1997). Bondage in time: Footbinding and fashion theory. *Fashion Theory*, 1 (1), 3–28.

Koda, H. (2005). Introduction. In H. Koda & A. Bolton (eds) *Chanel: Catalogue for the Metropolitan Museum of Art Exhibition* (pp. 11–12). New Haven, New Jersey: Yale University Press.

Kroeber, A. (1919). On the principle of order in civilization as exemplified by changes in fashion. *American Anthropologist*, 21, 235–263.

Kuchta, D. M. (2007). "Graceful, virile, and useful": The origins of the three-piece suit. In A. Reilly & S. Cosbey (eds) *The Men's Fashion Reader* (pp. 498–511). New York: Fairchild Books.

Kuhn, T. (1970). *The Structure of Scientific Revolutions* (2nd edition). Chicago: The University of Chicago Press.

Kvavadze E., Bar-Yosef, O., Belfer-Cohen, A., Boaretto, E., Jakeli, N., Matskevich, Z., & Meshveliani, T. (2009). 30,000-year-old wild flax fibers. *Science, 325* (5946):1359.

Lang, K., & Lang, G. E. (2007) The power of fashion. In L. Welters & A. Lillethun (eds) *The Fashion Reader* (pp. 83–86). Oxford: Berg.

Laughlin, J. (1997). A series of response papers. *Clothing and Textiles Research Journal, 15*(3), 162–163.

Laver, J. (1973). Taste and fashion since the French Revolution. In G. Willis & D. Midgley (eds) *Fashion Marketing* (pp. 379–389). London: George Allen & Unwin.

Laver, J. (1937). *Taste and Fashion.* London: Dood Mead and Co.

Laver, J. (1969). *Modesty in Dress: An Inquiry into the Fundamentals of Fashion.* Boston: Houghton Mifflin Company.

Leibenstein, H. (1950). Bandwagon, snob, and Veblen effects in the Theory of Consumers' Demand. *Quartlery Journal of Economics, 64,* 183–207.

Levi Strauss & Co. The Rivet Patent, May 20, 1873. (1873, June 28). *Pacific Rural Press,* p. 406.

Lillethun, A. (2007). Introduction [to Part II: Fashion Theory] in L. Welters & A. Lillethun (eds) *The Fashion Reader* (pp. 77–86). Oxford: Berg.

Lipovetsky, G. (1994). *The Empire of Fashion: Dressing Modern Democracy.* Trans. Catherine Porter. Princeton, NJ: Princeton University Press.

Lipovetsky, G. (2005). *Hypermodern Times.* Cambridge, MA: Polity Press.

Lowe, E. D, & Lowe, J. W. (1982). Cultural pattern and process: A study of sylistic change in women's dress. *American Anthropologist, 84* (3), 521–544.

Lowe, E. D., & Lowe, J. W. (1985). Quantitative analysis of women's dress: Implication for theories of fashion. In M. R. Solomon (ed.) *The Psychology of Fashion* (pp. 193–206). Lexington, MA: D. C. Heath.

Lowe, E., & Lowe, J. (1990). Velocity of the fashion process in women's formal evening dress. *Clothing and Textiles Research Journal, 9* (1), 50–58.

Mabry, M. A. (1971). The relationship between fluctuations in hemlines and stock market average from 1921 to 1971. Thesis. University of Tennessee, Knoxville.

Martin, J. J., Kibler, A., Kulinna, P. H., & Fahlman, M. (2006). Social physique anxiety and muscularity and appearance cognitions in college men. *Sex Roles, 55,* 151–158.

Maslow, A. (1943). A theory of human motivation. *Psychological Review, 50*(4), 370–396.

Matkovi , V. (2010). The power of fashion: The influence of knitting design on the development of knitting technology. *Textile, 8* (2), 122–147.

McCracken, G. (1988). *Culture and Consumption.* Bloomington, Indiana: Indiana University Press.

McLennan, J. F. (1869). The worship of animals and plants part 1. *Fortnightly Review, 6,* 407–427, 562–582.

McLennan, J. F. (1870). The worship of animals and plants part 2. *Fortnightly Review, 7,* 194–216.

McCurdy, D. W., Spradley, J. P., & Shandy, D. J. (2004). *The Cultural Experience: Ethnography in Complex Society* (2nd edition). Long Grove, Illinois: Waveland Press.

Mead, G. H. (1967). *Mind, Self, and Society: From the Standpoint of a Social Behaviorist (Works of George Herbert Mead, Vol. 1).* Edited by Charles W. Morris. Chicago, Illinois: University of Chicago Press.

Melichor-Bonnet, S. (2001). *The Mirror: A History.* New York: Routledge.

Merriam-Webster Dictionary (2013a). Theory. Downloaded December 2, 2013 from http://www.merriam-webster.com/dictionary/theory

Merriam-Webster Dictionary (2013b). Fashion. Downloaded June 28, 2013 from http://www.merriam-webster.com/dictionary/fashion

Merriam, S. B. (1988). *Case Study Research in Education: A Qualitative Approach*. San Francisco: Jossey-Bass.

Miller, K. A. (1997). Dress: Private and secret self expression. *Clothing and Textiles Research Journal*, *15* (4), 223–234.

Miller-Spillman, K. A. (2008). Male Civil War reenactors's dress and magical moments. In A. Reilly and S. Cosbey (eds) *The Men's Fashion Reader* (pp. 455–473). New York: Fairchild Books.

Miller-Spillman, K. A. (2013) Fashion and fantasy. In K. A. Miller-Spillman, A. Reilly, & P. Hunt-Hurst *Meanings of Dress* 3rd edition (pp. 469–469). New York: Fairchild Books.

Misener, J. (2011). Coco Rocha: I was told to "look anorexic.' The Huffington Post. Downloaded on May 11, 2013 from http://www.huffingtonpost.com/2011/12/08/coco-rocha-anorexic_n_1137116.html

Morgado, M. (1996). Coming to terms with Postmodern: Theories and concepts of contemporary culture and their implications for apparel scholars. *Clothing and Textiles Research Journal*, *14* (1), pp. 41–53.

Morgado, M. (2007). The semiotics of extraordinary dress: A structural analysis and interpretation of hip-hop style. *Clothing and Textiles Research Journal*, *25* (2), 131–155.

Morgado, M. (in press). Fashion phenomena and the post-postmodern condition: A speculative inquiry. *Fashion, Style & Popular Culture*

Musgrave, E. (2009). *Sharp Suits*. London: Pavilion Books.

Nag, D. (1991). Fashion, gender, and the Bengali middle class. *Public Culture*, *3* (2), 93–112.

National Association of Anorexia Nervosa and Associated Disorders. (n.d.) Eating disorder statistics. Downloaded May 27, 2013 from http://www.anad.org/get-information/about-eating-disorders/eating-disorders-statistics/

Negrin, L. (2008). Body art and men's fashion. In A. Reilly & S. Cosbey (eds) *The Men's Fashion Reader* (pp. 323–336). New York: Fairchild.

Niessen, S. (2007). Re-orienting fashion theory. In L. Welters & A. Lillethun (eds). *The Fashion Reader* (pp. 105–110). Oxford: Berg.

North, S. (2008). Fashion and politics: ". . . a son of liberty will not feel the coarseness of a homespun shirt . . ." In A. Reilly & S. Cosbey (eds) *The Men's Fashion Reader* (pp 180–198). New York: Fairchild.

Nystrom, P. H. (1929). *Economics of Fashion*. New York: Ronald Press.

O'Cass, A., & McEwen, H. (2004). Exploring consumer status and conspicuous consumption. *Journal of Consumer Behaviour*, *4* (1), 25–39.

Pannabecker, R. K. (1996). "Tastily bound with ribands": Ribbon-bordered dress of the Great Lakes Indians, 1735–1839. *Clothing and Textiles Research Journal*, *14* (4), 267–275.

Partington, A. (1992). Popular fashion and working-class affluence. In J. Ash & E. Wilson (eds) *Chic Thrills: A Fashion Reader* (pp. 145–161). London: Pandora.

Pedersen, E. L. (2001). Men's head and facial hair in the Far West: 1873–1899. *Clothing and Textiles Research Journal*, *19* (4), 185–190.

Pepys, S. (1972). *The Diary of Samuel Pepys* (Vol. 7), R. Latham (ed.). London: G. Bell and Sons.

Phau, I., & Ong, D. (2007). An investigation of the effects of environmental claims in promotional messages for clothing brands. *Marketing Intelligence and Planning*, *25*, 772–778.

Polhemus, T. (1994). *Streetstyle: From Sidewalk to Catwalk*. London: Thames & Hudson.

Polhemus, T. (2011). *Fashion & Anti-Fashion: Exploring Adornment and Dress from an Anthropological Perspective*. Publisher: Author.

Pope, H. G., Jr., Phillips, K. A., & Olivardia, A. (2000). *The Adonis Complex: The Secret Crisis of Male Body Obsession*. New York: Free Press.

Poysden, M., & Bratt, M. (2006). *A History of Japanese Body Suit Tattooing*. Amsterdam, Netherlands: KIT Publishers.

Reilly, A. (2008). Fashion cycles in men's jackets, dress shirts, and slacks. In A. Reilly & S. Cosbey (eds) *The Men's Fashion Reader* (pp. 525–537). New York: Fairchild Books.

Reilly, A. (in work). The theory of Shifting Erogenous Zones: Tattoos and the male body.

Reilly, A., & Rudd, N. A. (2009). Social anxiety as predictor of personal aesthetic among women. *Clothing and Textiles Research Journal*, *27* (3), 227–239.

Richardson, J., & Kroeber, A. (1940). Three centuries of women's dress fashions. *Anthropological Records*, *5* (2), 111–153.

Roach-Higgins, E., & Eicher, J. B. (1992). Dress and identity. *Clothing and Textiles Research Journal*, *10* (4), 1–8.

Robinson, D. E. (1976). Fashions in shaving and trimming of the beard: The men of the *Illustrated London News*, 1842–1972. *American Journal of Sociology*, *81* (5), 1133–1141.

Rogers, E. M. (1962). *Diffusion of Innovations*. New York: The Free Press.

Rudd, N. A., & Lennon, S. J. (2000). Body image and appearance-management behaviors in college women. *Clothing and Textiles Research Journal*, *18* (3), 152–162.

Saethre, E. (2012). (A. Reilly, Interviewer)

Saethre, E. (2013). Much more than plastic: Reflections on building *Star Wars* Stormtrooper armor. In K. A. Miller-Spillman, A. Reilly, and P. Hunt-Hurst (eds) *Meanings of Dress* (3rd edition) (pp. 495–500). New York: Fairchild Books.

Samuels, R. (2008). Auto-modernity after postmodernism: Autonomy and automation in culture, technology and education. In T. McPherson (ed.), *Digital Youth, Innovation, and the Unexpected* (pp. 219–240). Cambridge, MA: The MIT Press.

Sapir, E. (1931). Fashion. *Encyclopedia of the Social Sciences*. Volume 6. New York: Macmillan.

Saussure, F. de (1966). *Course in General Linguistics* (W. Baskin, Trans.). New York: McGraw-Hill.

Schildkrout, E. (2001). Body art as visual language. *AnthroNotes*, *22* (2). Accessed November 27, 2013 from http://anthropology.si.edu/outreach/anthnote/Winter01/anthnote.html

Shiveley, D. (n.d.). Bakufu versus Kabuki. *Harvard Journal of Asiatic Studies*, 326–356.

Simmel, G. (1904). Fashion. *International Quarterly*, *10*, 130–150.

Skoggard, I. (1998). Transnational commodity flows and the global phenomenon of the brand. In A. Brydon & S. Niessen (eds) *Consuming Fashion: Adorning the Transnational Body* (pp. 57–70). Oxford: Berg.

Slade, T. (2009). *Japanese Fashion: A Cultural History*. Oxford: Berg.

Solomon, M. R. (1985). *The Psychology of Fashion*. Lexington, Massachusetts: Lexington Books.

Solomon, M. R., & Rabolt, N. J. (2004). *Consumer Behavior in Fashion*. Upper Saddle River, New Jersey: Pearson Education/Prentice Hall.

Sparke, P. (1986). *An Introduction to Design and Culture in the Twentieth Century*. New York: Routledge.

Sproles, G. (1985). Behavioral science theories of fashion. In M. R. Solomon (ed.) *The Psychology of Fashion* (pp. 55–70). Lexington, Massachusetts: Lexington Books.

Sproles, G. B. (1979). *Fashion: Consumer Behavior Toward Dress*. Minneapolis: Burgess.

Sproles, G. B. & Burns, L. D. (1994). *Changing Appearances: Understanding Dress in Contemporary Society*. New York: Fairchild.

Stanley, T., & Danko, W. (1996). *The Millionaire Next Door*. New York: Pocket Books.

Steele, V. (1985). *Fashion and Eroticism: Ideals of Feminine Beauty from the Victorian Era to the Jazz Age*. Oxford: Oxford University Press.

Steele, V. (1998). *Paris Fashion: A Cultural History* (2nd ed.) Oxford: Berg.

Steele, V. (2002) Fashion: Yesterday, today, tomorrow. In N. White & I. Griffiths (eds) *The Fashion Business: Theory, Practice, Image* (pp. 7–22). Oxford, Berg.

Stitziel, J. (2005). *Fashioning Socialism: Clothing, Politics and Consumer Culture in East Germany*. Oxford: Berg.

Stone, G. P. (1965). Appearance and the self. In M. E. Roach & J. B. Eicher (eds) *Dress, Adornment and the Social Order* (pp. 216–245). New York: John Wiley & Sons.

Svendsen, L. (2006). *Fashion: A Philosophy*. Trans. John Irons. London: Reaktion Books.

Taylor, L. (2000). The Hilfiger factor and the flexible commercial world of couture. In N. White & I. Griffiths (eds) *The Fashion Business: Theory, Practice, Image* (pp. 121–142). Oxford: Berg.

Tricarico, D. (2008). Dressing up Italian Americans for the youth spectacle: What difference does Guido perform? In A. Reilly & S. Cosbey (eds) *The Men's Fashion Reader* (pp. 265–277). New York City: Fairchild.

Tseëlon, E. (2010). Outlining a fashion studies project. *Critical Studies in Fashion and Beauty, 1* (1), 3–53.

Tu, R. (2009). Dressing the nation: Indian cinema costume and the making of a national fashion, 1947–1957. In E. Paulicelli & H. Clark (eds) *The Fabric of Cultures: Fashion, Identity, and Globalization* (pp. 28–40). New York City: Routledge.

Vanhaeren, M., d'Errico, F., van Niekerk, K. L., Henshilwood, C. S., & Erasmus, R. M. (2013) Thinking strings: Additional evidence for personal ornament use in the Middle Stone Age at Blombos Cave, South Africa. *Journal of Human Evolution, 64,* 500–517.

Veblen, T. (1899). *The Theory of the Leisure Class*. New York: Macmillan.

Wade, T. D., Keski-Rahkonen A. & Hudson, J. (2011). Epidemiology of eating disorders. In M. Tsuang and M. Tohen (eds) *Textbook in Psychiatric Epidemiology* (3rd edition) (pp. 343–360). New York: Wiley.

Welters, L., & Lillethun, A. (2007). *The Fashion Reader*. Oxford: Berg.

Wikipedia. (2013). Theory. Downloaded December 2, 2013 from http://en.wikipedia.org/wiki/Theory

Wilson, E. (1987). *Adorned in Dreams: Fashion and Modernity*. Berkeley and Los Angeles: University of California Press.

Winter K., & McDermott, N. (2013). Is the hourglass figure a thing of the past? Women's waists have grown 7 INCHES since 1951 while weight soars by 7.5 lbs. Mail Online. Downloaded May 20, 2013 from http://www.dailymail.co.uk/femail/article-2312861/Times-Mad-Men-hourglass-figures-Womens-waists-7-INCHES-bigger-1950s-weight-risen-7-5lbs.html

Vermeulen, T., & van der Akker, R. (2010). Notes on metamodernism. *Journal of Aesthetics and Culture, 2,* 1–14.

Wallender, M. (2012, July 3). T-shirt blues: The environmental impact of a t-shirt. *The Huffington Post*.

Wilms, M. (Director). (2009). *Comrade Couture* [Motion Picture].

Wilson, E. (2003). *Adorned in Dreams* (2nd edition). New York: Rutgers University Press.

Wilson, L. (2008). The evolution of Western style in menswear. In A. Reilly & S. Cosbey (eds) *The Men's Fashion Reader* (pp. 465–479). New York City: Fairchild Books.

INDEX

aesthetic perception and learning 33, 38, 52, 71
Akubra 88–89
androgyny 22
ambivalence 48–49

Bloomers 74–75
Body 5, 6, 12, 13, 16, 17, 23, 25, 31, 33, 35–38, 40, 43, 44, 45, 49, 50, 52, 86–88, 91, 94, 96, 101, 102, 107, 109, 116, 123
body image 11, 33, 35–37, 52
bracelet 22–23, 65, 125
branding 17, 110–111, 116, 120

Casual Friday 64, 84, 86
La Chambre Syndicale de la Couture 101, 117
Chanel 64, 68, 71, 92, 94, 95, 111, 113, 119, 126
Chanel No. 5 95
classic 13–14, 27, 88, 105–106, 111, 126–127
conspicuous consumption 58, 68–70, 76–77
cowboy 11, 19, 26, 86, 87, 88
cultural authentication 12, 90–93, 98
cyborg 116

diamonds 21, 65, 76, 105
Dior 8, 37, 39, 46, 64, 68, 81, 82, 101, 107, 111, 119
  see also New Look

Fad 13–14, 27, 126
Fashion communicators 33, 52
Fashion innovators 31–33, 52, 104, 121, 128

Fragrance 13, 51–53, 66, 68, 87, 95, 111
  see also Chanel No. 5
  see also perfume
France 46, 58, 72–75
fur 5, 15, 19, 59, 103, 107

Gap 68, 104, 112–113, 121
Germany 5, 48–49, 58, 79, 110
Gucci 66, 68, 101–111, 113, 120–121
Guido 86–87

Halston 66–67, 121
Hawai'i 47, 86, 91–93, 96
Hilfiger 122
historic continuity 12, 31, 33, 45, 52, 104, 119, 121–122
historic resurrection 57, 107, 117, 119

innovation 15, 70, 94–95, 104–107, 116–117, 120, 123
invidious consumption 70
Irezumi 44, 96–97, 120
irony 21, 88, 90

Japan 16, 59, 92, 94, 96–97, 105, 109, 120
jewelry 13, 21, 31, 65, 72, 95, 106, 109, 111, 120, 128
  see also bracelet
  see also diamonds
  see also pearls

Keffiyeh scarf 125

logo 40, 66, 11–13, 121

market infrastructure 102, 117, 122
meme 26–27, 75

midi skirt 121–122
modern 6, 14, 15, 19–22, 27–28, 59, 61, 92,
    94, 95, 96, 98

New Look 8, 39, 81–82, 107, 110–120
    see also Dior

questioning 20–22, 28

pearls 38, 70, 95, 105–106
perfume 10, 95, 120
planned obsolescence 13, 27
postmodern 3, 19–23, 27–28, 62, 88,
    109, 120
post-postmodern 19, 23, 27, 28, 120
Public, Private, Secret Self model 4,
    33–34,52

Ralph Lauren 88, 104, 109, 122

Sans Culottes 72–74
sari 16, 49–50
scarcity 57, 64–65, 76
semiotic 16, 19–20, 28, 47, 71

shoes 6, 13, 18–20, 23, 28–29, 44, 56, 66,
    70, 75, 108, 126–127
shifting erogenous zones 33, 40, 43–45,
    52–53, 120–121
spatial diffusion 84–86, 96–98, 120
status consumption 51
suit 3, 15, 25, 34–35, 39, 58–59, 64, 71–72,
    81, 96, 109, 111
symbolic interaction 33, 47, 49, 52

tattoo 2, 6, 12, 16, 23, 32, 36, 44–45,
    96–97, 116, 125
    see also Irezumi
technology 12, 14, 23, 80–81, 84, 86, 92,
    94, 98, 102, 104–107, 116–117
Teddy Boy 59–61, 86
trickle across 57, 103, 117
trickle down 6, 57–62, 76–77, 84,94, 103,
    119, 121
trickle up 57, 62–64, 77, 103, 120–121

Yakuza 96–7, 120

Zeitgeist 56, 801, 87, 98m 107, 120 126, 128

CPSIA information can be obtained at www.ICGtesting.com
Printed in the USA
LVOW09s1531100216

474529LV00008B/197/P